'A CONCERN IN TRADE'

'A Concern in Trade'

Hatting and the Bracebridges of Atherstone, 1612–1872

JUDY VERO

Warwickshire Books, 1995

First published in 1995 by Warwickshire Books,
an imprint of Warwickshire County Council,
Department of Libraries and Heritage,
Barrack Street, Warwick CV34 4TH.

ISBN 1-871942-15-2

Typeset by Carnegie Publishing, 18 Maynard St, Preston
Printed and bound by Redwood Books, Trowbridge, Wilts

Contents

List of Illustrations

Acknowledgements

Fɪʀsᴛ ᴀɴᴅ ꜰᴏʀᴇᴍᴏsᴛ thanks are due to Mr Christopher Jeens, Warwickshire County Archivist, for editing the text and helping with interpretation of the legal documents. I am particularly grateful to Dr Marilyn Palmer of the University of Leicester, who encouraged me to write the book and corrected the first draft. Also to Mr John Austin for comments and corrections, and to Mr Christopher Foster who read a later draft. For transcriptions of probate material I am indebted to the Atherstone Local History Research Group, and in particular Mrs Marion Alexander, whose work on Atherstone in the sixteenth and seventeenth centuries has been an invaluable source. For help on Hartshill's history I must thank Mrs Joan Allen, and, for assistance with the Wilday family history, Mr Barry Withers. Thanks also to Mrs Fiona Donnelly for the use of the Vero family papers, and the Worshipful Company of Feltmakers of London, for use of the records in the Guildhall Library. A special thanks to the staff of the Warwickshire County Record Office, who never fail to be helpful and courteous, whatever the request. Last but by no means least, thanks to Vero & Everitt Ltd for sponsorship, and to my husband, Howard Vero, for his encouragement and support.

1. Avins Yard on the south side of Long Street. An example of the yard habitation which developed from the late eighteenth century to accommodate immigrant hatters.

CHAPTER I

Setting The Scene

O N A CLEAR DAY, the market town of Atherstone[1] can be seen to good advantage from the site of an Iron Age fort which crowns a hill to the south-east. Said to be the highest point in Warwickshire, this lofty vantage point has been valued by man for millennia. To the west lies the Arden, a landscape of cosy fields and woodlands, marked out by dense holly hedges and deep lanes, their banks bright with bluebells and primroses in spring. To the east, the wide panorama of Leicestershire countryside stretches out as far as the eye can see, a flat patchwork of fields and fox coverts, studded with spires and towers.

Between these contrasting landscapes, the eye focusses on Atherstone, a medley of ancient and modern roof tops, lining Roman Watling Street, bounded on the north by the meandering River Anker, and on the south by the Coventry Canal and the Trent Valley Railway line. Until the middle of the present century the population of this town was crowded into cramped tenements in narrow yards, some of the worst slums in all England. The stale air was heavy with the stench of privy and ashpit, making them breeding grounds for disease. From the pinched entrances of these fetid yards, the inhabitants could only gaze upon the green fields and expansive acres of the neighbouring gentry.

From the east in early times had come Danish invaders who did not risk pressing their conquest up into the Arden but halted at Watling Street, leaving their Anglo-Saxon adversaries safe in the woodland villages to the west. The Danes made their own settlements on the east of Watling Street.[2] Confronting each other across this busy thoroughfare, the two cultures are said to have met in a gruesome game, where the object was

---

[1] Warwickshire County Record Office (W.C.R.O.) and Lichfield Joint Record Office file all documents under the parish name of Mancetter which contained four manors, Mancetter, Atherstone, Hartshill and Oldbury.

[2] This can be seen in village names. In the wooded Arden to the south-west of Watling Street are the '-ley' villages, Anglo-Saxon for 'clearing in the wood'. To the east are the '-bys' and 'thorpes', which indicate Danish settlement.

to win a severed head. The tradition continues on Shrove Tuesday each year, a large leather football replacing the head.

Domesday Book gives the first indication that Atherstone might later become the location of a rural industry, for the people had an unusual degree of independence for feudal times. The eleven villeins who farmed the land in 1086, represented 79% of the population, which is well above the Warwickshire average of 57%.[3] These men were not free, but they were not badly off. They had a certain amount of autonomy in running their farms, visited only from time-to-time by the steward of their feudal landlord, the Earl of Chester. Used to minimal supervision, they became more independent and less servile than their more closely governed counterparts in the villages of the Warwickshire Feldon to the south. This was the legacy they would pass on to future generations. Such independence has been seen as a characteristic of the heavily wooded Arden, where settlements were larger, the forest less penetrable, and a variety of industries later became established. In the twelfth century the manor of Atherstone passed into the hands of the Abbot of Bec from France, who laid out burgages, but did not win borough status for the town. The villeins took advantage of their absentee landlord and his lenient stewards, claiming that they were unjustly treated.[4] The evidence does not support their claim, for compared to other holdings of the Abbot of Bec, the labour services required at Atherstone were light, perhaps inadequate for the size of the demesne. Successive abbots struggled on against their insubordinate subjects until the late fourteenth century, when the Abbot tried unsuccessfully to lease the manor to the neighbouring Cistercian house at Merevale. After the suppression of the alien houses, the manor passed through a succession of absentee landlords. Meanwhile, the erstwhile villeins took advantage of the situation, acquiring the demesne lands for themselves, and becoming freeholders.[5]

Increasing freedom of activity encouraged an independence of spirit in the townsfolk, and, in the sixteenth century, drew newcomers who wished to share in the good life the town offered. Some of these newcomers were craftsmen. They were following a general trend in fleeing from large towns and cities to be free from the petty restrictions imposed on them by powerful guilds and corporations. In the country they could work in freedom, without interference. But the countryside did not offer bucolic delights to the craftsmen. Much of the land had been worked for centuries,

---

[3] B. Watts and E. Winyard, *The History of Atherstone* (Keele, 1988), p. 8.

[4] M. Morgan, *The English Lands of the Abbey of Bec* (Oxford, 1946), p. 91.

[5] Morgan, p. 118.

if not the full span of human history, and the number of mouths it could feed was strictly limited. Rather than discarding the hammer or the awl to take up the hoe or the harrow, the craftsman had to depend upon his former trade to feed his family. The fruit of his craft, whether shoes or wheels, coats or caps, was sold at the market to buy food. These craftsmen added to the wealth of skills which made the towns and villages of rural England self-sufficient at that time.

Whilst the population was rising steadily, and the land available for feeding that population remained constant, there had to be some changes in the traditional way of life of rural communities. Not only did the immigrant population have to continue with its craft skills to survive, but some of the indigenous population, too, began to change from husbandry to industry to make ends meet. Thus another reason emerges for the establishment of a rural industry, for studies show that, where a growing population pressed hard upon the land, industry would find a home.[6]

In Atherstone, despite generous commons, the land available for cultivation had remained constant since the days when the Abbot of Bec held the manor. By 1547 there was a shortage of arable land and commons, creating a situation which caused concern for the Lord of the Manor, Henry, Marquis of Dorset. His surveyors pointed out that the major landholder of the town, Amias Hill, held sixty-three acres, which were:

> In the occupacion of dyverse pore men as well husbanndmen as artyfycers of the towne. And when so ever they shall come to the lordes hannd to be lette or sett yt shall not be mete to demyse theym all to one man but to many and the mo the better bothe for the upholding of the towne and also for the lordes ffyne. And yf the lorde shall at any tyme suffre theis acres to be inclosed at the suyte of any man or for any ffyne yt wylbe an undoing to the towne not only for lacke of tyllage wherof they have lytle as may appeyre by this survey but also for lacke of comens wherof they have none but only the outwoodes whiche is in maner nothing worthe.[7]

The 'lacke of tyllage' was likely to be the result of soil exhaustion, and would have encouraged the population to look for ways of supplementing its income. As the surveyors report, in 1547 there was already a number of 'artyfycers' who were supplementing a living from the land with some

---

[6] J. Thirsk, 'Industries in the Countryside', in *Essays in the Economic and Social History of Tudor and Stuart England*, ed. F. J. Fisher (Cambridge, 1961), pp. 70–88.

[7] Survey of Henry, Marquis of Dorset, Manor of Atherstone 1547: L2/86, W.C.R.O.; Dugdale Papers: Court Rolls, 1334–1601, MR13, W.C.R.O.

sort of trading activity. The probate inventories of the sixteenth and seventeenth centuries show a gradual change from a mixed economy to the dominance of trade as the major means of livelihood.[8] Many of those families which made the transition from husbandry to trade were long established, and, over generations, we can witness the effects of soil exhaustion in the decline of their farming interest and the increase of their trading activity.[9]

The first industry to become established in Atherstone in the early modern period was tanning. Tanners provided the raw materials for local shoemakers, cordwainers and saddlers. Tanneries were built beside the watercourses, and when the trade declined in the eighteenth century, the hatters took over their premises. There was a small cloth industry, too. Woven cloth is a frequent item on the probate lists, and 'Tenter flatt' in the open fields was obviously indicative of an area where cloth was stretched out to dry.[10]

Although soil exhaustion is an important factor in the establishment of a rural industry, there have to be other preconditions. In Nottinghamshire and Leicestershire, studies have shown that it was in the predominantly freehold villages that industry came to rest.[11] Villages dominated by one large house did not develop into industrial centres. In south Nottingham-shire, where framework knitting became established, out of twenty villages with one large house, none developed the industry. But a quarter of the ninety-five which had no large house became framework knitting villages.

As we have seen, Atherstone, was strongly freehold from medieval times, and had a number of medium-sized houses. In 1663 there were three, including that of the lord of the manor, Seabright Repington, whose family had risen to wealth through trade, as weavers. Another belonged to George Purefoy, a citizen and haberdasher of London. The third house belonged to Samuel Bracebridge, the first recorded haberdasher of hats in the parish.[12] Thus a predisposition towards trade amongst the influential was there long before the hatting industry became established.

It was also important that cottagers were not too fully occupied with

---

[8] See M. J. Alexander, 'Sixteenth-Century Probate Documents from Mancetter', *Warwickshire History*, Vol. VI, No. 4 (Winter, 1985/6), p. 122.

[9] The Drayton family, tanners, are a good example.

[10] A Plan of Atherston Feildes, Robert Hewitt, 1716, P7, W.C.R.O.

[11] A. Rogers, 'Rural Industries and Social Structure: The Framework Knitting Industry of South Nottinghamshire 1670–1840', *Textile History*, 12 (1981), p. 20.

[12] Ed. M. Walker, *Warwick County Records: Hearth Tax Returns, Vol. I: Hemlingford Hundred: Tamworth and Atherstone Divisions* (Warwick, 1957), pp. 239–79.

husbandry. There had to be some time in the day which could be set aside for the loom, or the stocking frame, or the feltmaker's kettle. Thus a rural craft industry often followed in the wake of a thriving dairy industry.[13] This was a sign of good grazing on generous commons, and a family who had enough time to spare, after tending their crops, to make butter and cheese for the market. Although Atherstone had a well organised open field system, with everyone involved to some degree in arable farming, the town was also famous for a cheese fair on September the 8th, which was, according to Daniel Defoe, one of the greatest in the country.[14] Today, the legacy is still apparent in the cheese chambers which can be seen on the upper floors of some farm houses. The probate inventories of the sixteenth and seventeenth centuries also record large numbers of cheeses amongst the effects of the deceased.[15]

Until recently it was thought that the prime reason for the establishment of hatting was the topography of Atherstone. This may now be seen as one of several contributing factors. The town lies on a flat plain beside the River Anker, which regularly overflows its banks in winter, making it fruitless territory for the rearing of sheep, which are prone to foot rot in damp conditions. Sheep were reared more easily on the adjacent hillside, where the Cistercian monks of Merevale Abbey had been successful wool producers. But, local wool, being too coarse, was never satisfactory for feltmaking, and consequently most of the feltmaker's raw material was imported.

A good supply of pure water was a necessity. In Atherstone it came from springs which rise on the wooded uplands of the Arden plateau to the south-west of the town. In the swift dash across Watling Street to the River Anker, the water does not accumulate impurities, and so becomes the one essential local ingredient of the feltmaker's craft. The hillside has only a thin layer of soil covering an outcrop of good quality coal. In places the coal lies so close to the surface that rabbit burrows are black. It required merely a strong arm and a coal pick to obtain fuel for the feltmaker's kettle. It is also thought that the lime trees which favour the area were a source of timber for hat blocks.[16]

Communications, too, were excellent. Atherstone was situated on one of the most important thoroughfares in the country. Thus craftsmen were

---

[13] J. Thirsk, pp. 70–88.

[14] D. Defoe, *A Tour Through the Whole Island of Great Britain*, ed. Pat Rogers (Middlesex, 1971), pp. 365, 407.

[15] Probate inventories for the Parish of Mancetter are held by Lichfield Joint Record Office. Transcriptions are by courtesy of Atherstone Local History Research Group.

[16] J. Allen, *Heardred's Hill: A History of Hartshill and Oldbury* (Nuneaton, 1982), p. 136.

in an ideal position to dispose of their products. As, until recent years, the motor coaches would make an overnight stop on their way from London to Scotland, giving their passengers the opportunity to patronise Atherstone's many small shops, so it was in former times. Drovers came with their cattle, plodding slowly to Smithfield Market. Coach travellers broke their journey in the town's inns whilst horses were changed. Wagons passed, laden with cloth bound for London. Even Daniel Defoe paused in Atherstone to visit the cheese fair.

It used to be thought that rural industry would only develop where raw materials were to hand. In the case of the cloth industry, this would be a supply of wool, a seam of fuller's earth, and a reliable flow of water. However, as early as the seventeenth century, it was observed that Leicestershire, Lincolnshire, Northamptonshire and Cambridgeshire, had the most wool but made the least cloth.[17]

The Romans thought nothing of transporting materials and goods across continents, some of which found their way from the Black Sea to Mancetter, and vice-versa. In England, a network of packhorse trails had been in existence since prehistoric times, and it was not difficult to transport wool from the area where it was grown to the area where it was required. In the Middle Ages the export of wool to the continent of Europe was the mainstay of the country's economy, and in later years it was not at all unusual for wealthy Yorkshire clothiers to buy their wool from the eastern counties.[18] Even small market towns were able to develop trading links with distant places. Transport was undeniably slow and hazardous, especially in winter, when river crossings ran high and mud lay deep over the road. But it was adequate, and vast quantities of raw materials were moved long distances on the backs of packhorses. Even in the early days, wool for feltmaking did not come from local sheep, but was imported from Spain, Portugal, France and the East.

It can be argued that there are many other towns and villages in Britain which have a topography suitable for feltmaking, but did not develop a hatting industry. So why did hatmaking come to Atherstone in particular? Thus we come to the remaining and most important precondition for the development of a rural industry. This is the accident of fate which brings an entrepreneur to a particular place at a particular time.

The rural entrepreneur needed special qualities.[19] He had to be sharp

---

[17] Thirsk, pp. 70–88.

[18] P. J. Bowden, *The Wool Trade in Tudor and Stuart England* (London, 1962), p. 68.

[19] P. Mathias, *The First Industrial Nation: An Economic History of Britain 1700–1914* (London, 1983), pp. 136–48.

enough to buy the best raw materials at the keenest prices. He had to be tough and resilient to cope with the stubborn cottage master and his wayward family, who would resist any interference with their chosen pattern of work. He would have to control the quality of the finished product and sell it at the right price. And at the end of the day, he would need to be a good judge of character to decide which customer could be trusted with credit and who should pay cash on the nail. The Bracebridges were all of these.

It is not possible to generalise about the social origins of the entrepreneurs. They had to be men of some substance who could finance their own enterprises, but they came from all backgrounds, ranging from dukes and bishops, to peasants. Much has been written about the part played by the protestant ethic in the rise of the industrial entrepreneur. Although George Fox, the founder of the Quakers, a group which fathered much of this country's nascent industry, was born in the neighbouring Leicestershire village of Fenny Drayton, Atherstone's earliest hatmaking entrepreneurs were not all dissenters. Indeed, the Bracebridge family numbered Anglican clergy amongst its ranks. The entrepreneurs were not a class, but a type, identified by vision and determination, rather than ancestry or religion. It was upon their success that the modern British economy was founded.

Of paramount importance was the entrepreneur's personality. It had to be strong, for a newcomer was unlikely to succeed if he came into conflict with a personality to equal his own. His success depended upon finding a weak manor with an absentee lord, and a large number of freeholders, who would not interfere with his plan. For, if the manor was strong it was likely that the lord would stamp out any budding industry. (This happened in two villages in Nottinghamshire in the 1840s, when the landowner cleared stockingers off his land.[20]) No landowner would stand by and watch the growth of an artisan population that derived its livelihood, not from himself, the traditional provider, but from a powerful intruder, who had no dynastically based authority in the locality. Furthermore, such a population was a threat to game and to the control of poor rates. In Atherstone, in the nineteenth century, the lord of the manor addressed both of these problems with one action. He had no power to rid himself of the thriving hat industry on his doorstep, so he solved the problem of poachers by building a ten-foot wall between his estate and

---

[20] D. R. Mills, 'Rural Industries and Social Structure: Framework Knitters in Leicestershire, 1670–1851', *Textile History*, 13 (2) 1982, p. 188.

the town. It is said that he used out-of-work hatters as labour, so preventing an increase in the poor rate.

Having set the scene, one might ask whether it was, indeed, by accident that the Bracebridges came to Atherstone. The industrialist of today, looking to recruit a workforce to man a new factory is likely to mount a feasibility study, taking into account the socio-economic composition of the local population, the employment level, the accessibility to transport systems, and the attitude of the local authority. Some of these factors might well have been taken into consideration before Richard Bracebridge, father of Samuel, unpacked his belongings at 'Duffcoate Shop' in the Market Place. He would have noted that the cottage labourer was under employed on the land, but struggling to feed his family. He would also have known that the lord of the manor rarely came near the town, and maintained a country seat elsewhere. For his own part, he would have established commercial links with distant markets, and would have known exactly how to exploit the predicament of an impoverished, yet growing, population.

Thus, the case of Atherstone offers a copy book example of the economic conditions which lead to the development of rural industry. But this is only part of the story. Although the Bracebridges were a colourful and domineering family who exploited the local population for their own economic benefit, they did not achieve all of their aims. Because Atherstone was renowned for generous commons, people were drawn to the town to take advantage of the common rights which were attached to the houses, and there was no incentive to enclose the land. In the mid-eighteenth century, with the proceeds of his trading interests, Abraham Bracebridge II purchased most of the town's arable land, and tried to obtain an act of parliament to enclose the open fields. But his attempt was frustrated by the townsfolk, who refused to give up their common rights and fought a long and hard battle against enclosure. Considering that Bracebridge's hatting business provided work for many of the cottagers, and this was an age when grassroots opinion generally counted for nothing, the achievements of the Atherstone people are extraordinary. It is a tribute to their tenacity that they managed to delay enclosure from the first attempt in 1738 until 1765.

It may be an accident of fate which brings a particular industry to a particular place, but once established, that industry shapes the character of the area, so that, over generations, it becomes impossible to imagine that any other could have taken its place. So it is with Atherstone, whose modern history has been shaped by the hatting trade. In the early days, being seasonal work, it complemented agricultural activity, and allowed cottage labourers a flexibility which suited their independent nature. Later on, when coal mining became the major industry, hatmaking was still able to fit in between the seasonal requirements of the coal master. Hat factories grew up where street and brook intersected. The burgage plots running along the Watling Street were gradually subdivided and developed with cramped tenements, to house the growing numbers of hatters.

Were it not for a road sign, erected by the county council to attract tourists, no visitor to the town today would know of Atherstone's history of hatmaking. Only one factory survives, and it is not in a prominent location. But for those who carry the tradition in their blood, it is impossible to deny. Hatting is still part of the local culture, deep in the memory of people, though hidden from the casual visitor.

Of course, Atherstone was not the only town where wool felt hatting developed. There were many others, though none survive in Britain today. Of the other areas where hatting thrived in earlier times, the most notable were the counties of Lancashire and Cheshire, where feltmaking co-existed with clothmaking. In the west, Frampton Cotterell, near Bristol, was another important hatmaking centre, close to the prosperous west of England cloth industry. At Rugeley in Staffordshire there was one centre of the trade which was almost the mirror of Atherstone, in size and topography. This town had an important wool felt hat industry, which co-existed with coal mining, but died out early in the nineteenth century.

Although the part played by religion in the development of feltmaking is unclear, the fact that Atherstone did not have a parish church of its own was significant. The town had to be content with a small chapel of ease. Marriages, baptisms and funerals were conducted at the parish church in Mancetter, a mile away, a minor settlement and centre of a large rural parish, which encompassed four manors. Because the influence of the established church was weak, it was to be expected that, when the dissenting church arose, it claimed a strong following in Atherstone, particularly amongst the hatters.

So we come again to the Bracebridges. Nothing remains of them in the town today, save a street name and a few acres of land which still belong to the family. For six generations the Bracebridges resided at Atherstone Hall, which lay on a pleasant incline overlooking the River Anker. Since it was first built in 1619, the house had, over time, been modelled and remodelled at the whim of fashion. In its last years, it was clothed in the stucco and classical detail, though perhaps not the true elegance, of the Regency period. By the 1960s Atherstone Hall had been split into flats, one of which provided a modest home for a last female descendant of the Bracebridges. Struggling with the problems of plumbing, maintenance and the idiosyncrasies of her tenants, Mrs Hanmer, a kindly lady, did not enjoy a blessed old age. At her death, apart from a lukewarm enquiry from the district council, there was no commercial interest in the rambling and unexceptional house, and it was soon sold to a developer who pulled it down in favour of a housing estate. It was an inauspicious end to a house and a family which had dominated the life of a small market town for over three hundred years.

2. Atherstone Hall, shortly before demolition in 1964

CHAPTER 2

The Early History of Feltmaking

WHEN feltmaking began in England in the sixteenth century it was a new and sophisticated craft, introduced by Huguenot immigrants, who had been driven from the continent through fear of religious persecution. Feltmaking has been seen as 'One of the most important manufactures brought into England by the refugees'.[1] Until that period the only felted headwear made in Britain was the cap, which had served its humble purpose since at least the thirteenth century, protecting the peasant's head from the elements through the seasons of the year.

These felt caps were made very differently from later hats. Wool yarn was first knitted in the round on four needles. The knitted cap was then fulled or 'thickened' by hand, using clubs to beat the wool as it lay in a trough of water and fuller's earth. Water-powered fulling mills were in use in the late twelfth century, and were able to replace the considerable manpower required to felt long and heavy broadcloth.[2] However, they never seriously supplanted the old manual method because, whilst labour was cheap, it was not cost-effective to build fulling mills, and where water power was available, it was more likely to be used for grinding corn than fulling cloth.[3]

However, we do know that it became an established practice to thicken knitted woollen caps in fulling mills, because, in 1376 it was necessary to pass an ordinance forbidding it on the grounds that mechanical fulling impaired the quality of the cap.[4] Thirty years later the cappers were petitioning the Crown to request, not only that mechanised fulling should be forbidden, but also that it should be illegal to full caps by foot.[5]

---

[1] S. Smiles, *The Huguenots, their Settlements, Churches and Industries in England and Ireland* (London, 1867), p. 268.
[2] E. M. Carus-Wilson, *Medieval Merchant Adventurers* (London, 1954), p. 189.
[3] Richard Holt, 'Milling Technology in the Middle Ages: The Direction of Recent Research', *Industrial Archaeology Review*, Vol. XIII, No. 1 (Autumn, 1990), p. 57.
[4] H. T. Riley, *Memorials of London*, pp. 401–4 (quoted in *Victoria County History: Surrey*, Vol. II, 1905, p. 359).
[5] Carus-Wilson, pp. 187–8.

3. Fulling mills in use in a modern hat factory.

Trampling on the wool in the trough of fuller's earth, must have been something like treading grapes for wine making, and far less tiring than hammering by hand. It is difficult to decide whether these restrictions were imposed in the genuine interest of protecting the quality of the finished cap, or the jobs of the cappers. Whatever the case, the illegal practice continued for a hundred years and required an enactment of parliament to ban it.[6]

Ironically, the fulling mill, or stock, as it is more commonly known today, had to wait a further six hundred years before it was legally used to felt headwear. Driven by steam power, it was adopted by the feltmakers in the late nineteenth century, and can still be found in use in today's hat factories. Two heavy oak hammers are alternately raised and dropped on several dozen of wet wool hat forms in a trough. After an hour or so of pounding by the bare wet wood, the wool shrinks to a tight felt.

The felt cap was not always a modest article for the use of the poorer classes of society. Occasionally these caps were lavishly trimmed with

---

[6] Stat. 22 Edw. IV, c. 5 (quoted in *Victoria County History: Surrey,* Vol. II, 1905, p. 359).

costly materials to appeal to the rich. Early this century an example came to light when a church tower was being repaired at Little Sampford in Essex.[7] It was uncovered during the removal of masonry and, as the tower was built in 1350, it is believed that the cap, which in shape is much like a modern hat, was placed there at that time. The crown and brim, both of felt, were made separately and then sewn together, suggesting that it was created before the craft of making felt hats in one piece was learnt. The cap was trimmed with silk and embroidered with the finest needlework.

By the end of the fourteenth century, whilst the English cappers continued with their craft, the technique for making felt hats had been discovered abroad.[8] Haberdashers and merchants began to import hats to satisfy a growing demand from their rich clients. At first they arrived in dozens, and later in hundreds of dozens, from the fashionable cities of Italy, France and Flanders. One of the earliest recorded wearers of a hat was Chaucer's fourteenth-century merchant. The Ellesmere Manuscript pictures him, 'Hye on horse . . . Upon his head a Flaundryssh bever hat'[9] The merchant's hat, made of beaver fur with a high crown and a low sweeping brim, was lavishly trimmed with what appears to be ermine. On the prosperous merchant, this hat was certainly a mark of status.

Despite stong competition from the emergent hatters, caps continued to be made right up until the eighteenth century. But it became increasingly difficult to keep the old trade going, and successive monarchs brought in measures to try and protect the cappers. Local craftsmen in town and country capping centres were driven out of business by the new felt hats which flooded the market and played havoc with local economies.[10] Eventually Queen Elizabeth was persuaded to tackle the problem. In 1570 she decreed, in her fifth and strongest statute, that all her subjects over six years of age, excepting the 'nobility and persons of degree', must wear on Sundays and holy days a 'cap of wool knit thick and dressed in England'.[11] This came to be known as the 'Statute Cap'. But even a statute

---

[7] K. Finch, 'A Medieval Hat Rediscovered', *Textile History*, 14 (2) (1983), pp. 67–70.

[8] J. H. Smith, 'The Development of the English Felt and Silk Hat Trades 1500–1912' (University of Manchester, Ph.D., 1980), p. 8.

[9] G. Chaucer, 'Canterbury Tales: General Prologue', *The Complete Works of Geoffrey Chaucer*, ed. F. N. Robinson, 2nd edition (Oxford, 1957), p. 19, line 272.

[10] G. Unwin, *Industrial Organization in the Sixteenth and Seventeenth Centuries*, 2nd edition (London, 1963), p. 71.

[11] Stat. 13 Eliz. I, c. 19.

of royal decree could not turn the tide of fashion which was sweeping the country, and before long it had to be repealed.

It is generally accepted that the first felt hats were made in England by feltmakers from Rouen in France, who settled in Southwark at the beginning of the sixteenth century.[12] By 1542 felt hats were also being made in Norwich by Huguenot immigrants.[13] We can imagine the curiosity of the English as they watched these foreigners, who made hats, 'As well and as good as ever came out of France or Flanders or any other realm'. As if by magic they persuaded the carded wool to felt without any prior spinning and knitting. The local inhabitants gazed in wonder, and the immigrants, proud of their skills, showed the Englishmen how to do it for themselves, innocently giving away all their secrets. Once the men of Norwich had squeezed the immigrants dry of their knowledge, they turned on them, using the petty restrictions of their guild to drive them out of town.[14]

What were these secrets? How was it possible to make felt without first knitting the wool yarn into a piece? The first secret was in the wool itself. It was no use taking wool from the backs of northern sheep. In most cases this was too coarse and would not felt quickly. The breeds of sheep which thrive in arid climates and graze sparse pastures, produce a fine fibred wool with a scaly surface which felts easily. Thus, the best wool for hatmaking was, and still is, imported. This well illustrates Joan Thirsk's observation that the raw materials for a craft industry could be transported long distances to where they were required.[15]

One early importer of wool for hatmaking was a Portuguese merchant, Hector Nounez. In 1573 he obtained a licence from Queen Elizabeth, 'To be the sole importer from the dominions of the King of Spain of all manner of Spanish wrought and unwrought wool suitable for the making of hats and felts'.[16]

In the early days, wool from the whole fleece was used for feltmaking, but after the combing machine was invented in the eighteenth century, it became easy to separate the wool into two qualities, the 'tops' and the 'noils'. The tops were the longer fibres used for spinning, and the noils (the waste), too short for spinning, were ideal for feltmaking.

In the bow garret, often an upper room where men worked in cubicles

---

[12] Smith, p. 9.
[13] Smiles, p. 268.
[14] Smiles, p. 104.
[15] Thirsk, pp. 70–88.
[16] Stat. 15 Eliz. I, c. 66/1098, 8 June 1573.

4. The bow garret.

side by side the carded wool was first teased out into a fluffy mass using a feltmaker's bow.[17] This was an ashen staff, from five to seven feet long, with a string of catgut stretched its length. It was so heavy that it had to be suspended from the ceiling by a cord to support its weight. The feltmaker held the bow in his left hand over the wool, which was piled on a wattle hurdle. He then plucked the string rapidly with a wooden pin, held in his right hand, making a 'peculiar twanging noise'.[18] The fibres flew upwards and fell in equal thickness on the hurdle, to make a soft and fluffy layer, termed a 'batt'.

The fragile batt was carried carefully to the workroom and separated into two equal parts of a roughly triangular shape. They were each pressed gently, first against the hurdle, and then against a piece of oil cloth or

---

[17] There are several accounts of feltmaking processes in the eighteenth and nineteenth centuries. As these accounts refer to tools and materials which appear on probate inventories and other documents of the sixteenth century, it is reasonable to assume that the method changed very little over a period of 300 years. The two accounts which form the basis of this description are an article which first appeared in the *Universal Magazine* for April 1750, and was reprinted in full in the *Hatter's Gazette* in 1888. It was reproduced again in Smith, Chapter 3. A second account can be found in George Dodd, *Days at the Factories* (London, 1843), reprinted 1967, pp. 144–54.

[18] Dodd, p. 144.

5. An eighteenth-century planking shop.

leather, known as a 'hardening skin'. The second process was carried out at the 'bason', a little hearth or fireplace, raised three feet high with an iron plate laid over and exactly covering it.[19] The feltmaker would sprinkle water on the consolidated wool and press it against the hot plate, producing that familiar smell of damp woollens drying before a fire. After working the wool for a while it lost all its fluffiness and became thin and compressed, but remained in a triangular shape.

Next the two triangles, measuring half a metre in each direction, were folded together into a cone shape with a piece of cotton cloth placed inside to stop the two sides from felting together. The cone was of a double thickness with the two joins arranged on opposite sides so that there would be no weakness as it felted.

The double batt, compressed and ready for felting, now termed a 'hardened form', was taken to the 'walking plank'. This term dated back to the medieval capping days and is further evidence that fulling by foot in a trough of water and fuller's earth, although at times illegal, did indeed

---

[19] Smith, Chapter 3, p. 122.

become an established practice. The 'walking plank' was made of hard-wood, usually mahogany, and arranged in eight sections, sloping down towards and around a cauldron, or 'kettle', with an area of lead where the wood and kettle joined. Filled with water, the kettle was heated from below by a fire. Up to eight men could work together around the kettle, or 'at the plank' as it was said.

The feltmaker's shop was an unhealthy working environment. Steam billowed from the open kettle filled with water, close to boiling point, and infused with wine lees or sulphuric acid. The noxious vapour filled the workshop, polluting the lungs of the feltmaker. So hard and hot was his labour that he worked stripped to the waist and took frequent refreshment from the alehouse. When Queen Adelaide passed through Atherstone in the mid-nineteenth century, she was greatly offended by the sight of bare torsos which greeted her, when crowds of feltmakers rushed from their workshops to catch a glimpse of the dowager queen.[20]

The hat form was dipped into the hot liquor and worked on the plank. Using a 'feltmaker's pin', which resembled an iron rolling pin, the workman would repeatedly dip the rolled-up form into the dilute acid, rolling and unrolling, twisting and pressing. He would also rub the form with a piece of leather or wood tied to the palm of his hand. Considerable skill was needed to maintain the correct thickness at different points of the 'hood', as the felted form was termed. Eventually, after four or five hours work, the form would have shrunk to less than half its former size. It is not surprising that the feltmaker's hands were red and rough. No apprentice could become a man without a 'hatter's knob', the callous which developed on the forefinger.

Next, the hood was dried in the 'stove', a small room intensely heated with a charcoal fire. By now the felt was dense and strong and could be stretched into shape without risk of tearing. Stiffening and proofing was done with glue or gum from Seneca in Africa. It was extracted from the bark of trees and, in the seventeenth century, imported via Rotter-dam.[21] Other ingredients of the proof included resins and turpentine, producing a highly inflammable cocktail, which was the cause of many factory fires in the nineteenth century. A recipe which had been passed down from father to son, and was in use in 1852, combined shellac, naptha, sandric, mastic, resin and turpentine.[22] Shellac is still used today

---

[20] W. H. Sale, 'Atherstone Bye-Gones', Atherstone Archaeological Society and Field Club, reprinted from *Atherstone News*, Jan–Feb, 1918.

[21] Calendar of Treasury Books, 7 June, 1677; 3 Feb, 1679–80; 15 March, 1680–81.

[22] T. P. Gummer's Dye and Proof Recipes, 1853, Vero & Everitt Archive.

for this purpose. The workman brushed the stiffening substance over the surface, and was able to adjust the amount in different areas so that the brim could, if necessary, be given extra stiffening. After this the hat was stretched over a wooden block and steamed into shape. It was then ready for dyeing.

The cheaper wool, or 'country' felts, made in Atherstone, were dyed black using logwood, imported from Campeachy in Central America. It arrived in logs five or six feet long, and was shredded then mixed with salts and urine, and brought to the boil to make the dye. The hats were often dyed on blocks to keep their shape, a framework of hats hung on brass pegs being winched into the steaming dye vat. After a few minutes it was raised, then left to dry. This process was repeated several times over a long period so that the dye could fully penetrate the fibres. In the later period when the hat was dyed before blocking, the bodies, or hoods, were placed in the vat and stirred by an apprentice, using a long pole, to get an even dye.

Next the hat was washed to remove impurities and stoved once more. Then it was placed on the block again and brushed and polished to get a smooth nap. Last of all, the hat passed into the hands of the women who trimmed it with lining, leather and band.

In the cities, such as London, Norwich, or Chester, where the trade was organised by a guild, a master hatter would preside over the workshop which was part of his home. He was allowed to take two apprentices, who each served an average of seven years before making a trial piece and being accepted into the guild, so becoming journeymen. The master would often employ several journeymen. When a journeyman wished to set up as a master himself, he first had to complete a masterpiece and present it to the guild. If it was satisfactory the guild would admit him upon payment of a fee.

Having thought to make their homes in London and Norwich, the first immigrant feltmakers had not found a ready welcome. In the City of London the old capping trade was controlled by the Haberdashers' Company, who wished to include the new feltmakers under their jurisdiction.[23] But the immigrants preferred to be free to practise their craft as they wished, outside the city walls where rents were lower and they suffered less discrimination. They set up feltshops in Southwark and Bermondsey, where remnants of the trade can still be found today.

Those who were driven from Norwich, after they had been persuaded

---

[23] Unwin, pp. 130–5.

to give away their secrets, may have moved north, for Huguenot names can be found on the lists of admissions of feltmakers to the Freedom of the City of Chester.[24] Some may also have found their way to Bristol. But, within a generation or so, many feltmakers gave up the cities and moved to the nearby countryside, where there was no formal organisation of craftsmen and they could work as they pleased. Villages became known for their feltmaking activity, Denton, Hyde and Stockport in Cheshire; Frampton Cotterell in Somerset.[25] Here hatmaking was able to supplement a living from agriculture carried on in the seasons of the year when there was little work on the land. The hats were sent to the towns where they were sold to retailers, haberdashers or merchants. Part-time farming activity gave the feltmakers the independence and status to deal on equal terms with the merchants or haberdashers of hats.

In the city, restrictions on work became tighter as time went on. The record books of the Worshipful Company of Feltmakers of the City of London, which received its Charter from James I in 1604, list transgressions which were punished by fine.[26] Piecework, the weighing out of materials by the master, to be made up outside his workshop, was forbidden in London, but the common method of work in the country. The employment of country journeymen, who had probably not served a full

Although Huguenot immigrants had brought the new craft to Britain, when the indigenous population learned it and took it to the countryside the finer points were lost. The early feltmakers had made hats at a high standard, for rich customers, often from fur rather than wool. The country workers, on the other hand, satisfied demand from the poorer section of society. They restricted themselves to wool felt hats, or 'country felts', simply dyed in drab and black. At this level, the craft was within the reach of the poorest cottager. An open iron kettle, a fire, a wooden plank and a few handfuls of wool gleaned from the brambles, were the bare essentials. True, that it would be a laborious business creating a felt hood from coarse English wool, but if time was not important and the batt, rolled up in a piece of linen cloth, could be picked up in any spare moment and taken to the kettle, there was no reason why a poor living should not be augmented by the fruits of this long and hard labour. The felted hood could then be sold via a middleman to the haberdashers and hatters of the town for a penny or so.

In the city, restrictions on work became tighter as time went on. The record books of the Worshipful Company of Feltmakers of the City of London, which received its Charter from James I in 1604, list transgressions which were punished by fine.[26] Piecework, the weighing out of materials by the master, to be made up outside his workshop, was forbidden in London, but the common method of work in the country. The employment of country journeymen, who had probably not served a full

---

[24] Wills at Chester, quoted in Smith, Chapter 2.

[25] See J. S. Moore, *The Goods and Chattels of our Forefathers: Frampton Cotterell and District Probate Inventories, 1539–1804* (Chichester, 1976).

[26] Court Book of the Company of Feltmakers of London, Guildhall Library Ms 1570/2.

apprenticeship, and whose work was inferior, was forbidden, unless it was to make 'course felts'. It is small wonder that the country master was glad to be free of these petty restrictions. He could organise his own labour and that of his family as he pleased and as the seasonal requirements of the year dictated.

CHAPTER 3

Atherstone's First
Hatmaking Entrepreneurs

THE FORTUNES of many families ebb and flow over the generations. So it was with the Bracebridges, who came into Warwickshire in the twelfth century from a village in Lincolnshire which bore their name. Peter de Bracebridge, a baron of considerable military power, married into the Arden family, whom William the Conqueror had made overlords of the manor of Kingsbury, a few miles to the west of Atherstone. The Ardens had little success in producing male heirs, and when the manor passed to Peter's wife, Amicia, he became lord. However, his tenure was always disputed by the Ardens, and a few years later Thomas de Arden tried to claim back the estate, suggesting a duel to settle the matter. The Bracebridges were never eager to take up arms, preferring to use the law as weapon. In this case it served them well and John kept the estate.[1]

In the thirteenth century, his grandson, John de Bracebridge, joined the barons in revolt against Henry III, and was taken prisoner at the battle of Evesham in 1265. By paying a heavy fine he was able to keep his head. But the fine, five years revenue from his estate, crippled him financially and he was forced to lease out the land until the family was able to buy it back in 1301.

The Bracebridges joined the knighthood, and were soon in a position to increase their estates, leasing the manor of Sutton from the Earl of Warwick, on whose behalf Ralph Bracebridge mustered an army to serve Henry V at Agincourt.

The continuing feud with the Ardens came to a head in 1474, when John Arden fell in love with Alice Bracebridge, the daughter of Richard Bracebridge. John's father refused to consent to marriage, and Richard, greatly affronted by this, stormed the Arden house at Curdworth and abducted John. Such a story might well have influenced Shakespeare had

---

[1] W. Dugdale, *The Antiquities of Warwickshire*, 2nd Edition (Coventry, 1765), p. 747.

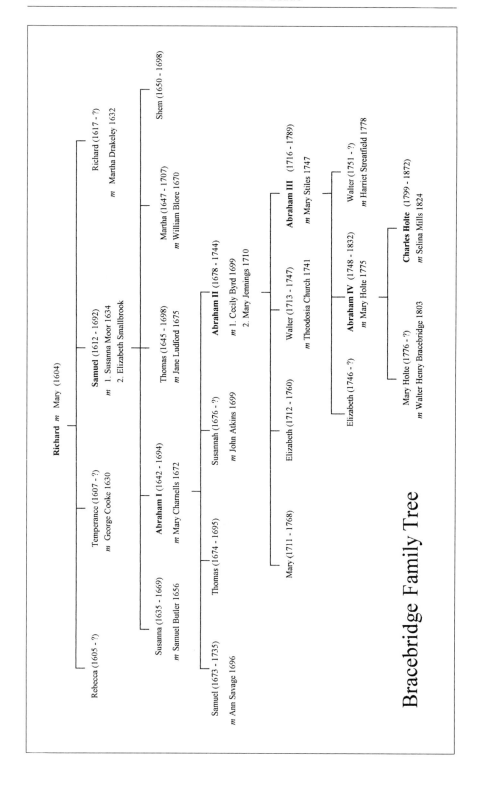

Richard *m* Mary (1604)

Rebecca (1605 - ?)

Temperance (1607 - ?)
m George Cooke 1630

Samuel (1612 - 1692)
m 1. Susanna Moor 1634
     2. Elizabeth Smallbrook

Richard (1617 - ?)
m Martha Drakeley 1632

Shem (1650 - 1698)

Susanna (1635 - 1669)
m Samuel Butler 1656

Abraham I (1642 - 1694)
m Mary Charnells 1672

Martha (1647 - 1707)
m William Blore 1670

Thomas (1645 - 1698)
m Jane Ludford 1675

Samuel (1673 - 1735)
m Ann Savage 1696

Thomas (1674 - 1695)

Susannah (1676 - ?)
m John Atkins 1699

Abraham II (1678 - 1744)
m 1. Cecily Byrd 1699
     2. Mary Jennings 1710

Mary (1711 - 1768)

Elizabeth (1712 - 1760)

Walter (1713 - 1747)
m Theodosia Church 1741

Abraham III (1716 - 1789)
m Mary Stiles 1747

Elizabeth (1746 - ?)

Abraham IV (1748 - 1832)
m Mary Holte 1775

Walter (1751 - ?)
m Harriet Streatfield 1778

Mary Holte (1776 - ?)
m Walter Henry Bracebridge 1803

Charles Holte (1799 - 1872)
m Selina Mills 1824

Bracebridge Family Tree

it not been for the fact that this couple, unlike their Italian counterparts, were soon happily married.

Their grandson, Thomas Bracebridge, was an extravagant man, who ran so deeply into debt that, in 1650, the manor had to be leased again, this time to Sir Ambrose Cave, Chancellor of the Duchy of Lancaster. Thomas died in 1569 and his son, Thomas, who was equally extravagant, converted the twenty-one year lease into 300 years for an annual rent of £42 4s. 3d. So ended the Bracebridges' influence in Kingsbury.

Thomas's brother, Anketil, married Ann Corbin of Hall End Hall, Dordon, near Atherstone. Her mother was the daughter of William Repington, a descendant of prosperous Atherstone weavers, whose family had acquired the manor of Amington, near Tamworth, and then, in 1607, the manor of Atherstone. There were four children of this marriage, the youngest of which, Richard, married in 1604 and settled in Atherstone.

Richard Bracebridge rented a modest copyhold property, 'Duffcoate Shop', near the market place, probably from his maternal grandparents, who, having risen in the world through trade, may well have encouraged him to go into trade himself. He would have served an apprenticeship, probably in Birmingham, which although a minor settlement at the time, was the location of a small property belonging to the Bracebridges. With the family fortunes dissipated, and needing to make his own way in the world, it was probably the only option open to him.

From his shop, near the bustling market place, Richard Bracebridge conducted his trade as a haberdasher. Today, when we think of haberdashers we are reminded of the shops of yesteryear, crammed with flat boxes, filled with a variety of small wares used in dressmaking: buttons, elastic, hooks and eyes, ribbons, buckram and binding tape. The haberdasher, knowledgeable about dressmaking and tailoring, would search willingly for the precise item the customer required, though it cost but a penny or two. In the sixteenth and seventeenth centuries, the haberdasher was in some ways similar. But, in addition to small wares, he would also be selling more costly items, such as hats, caps and gloves, imported from the fashionable centres of Europe. Sometimes the importation was on a huge scale. For example, in 1514, Thomas Heton of London applied for a 'licence to import 100 gross of French, Milanese or other caps, and 100 gross of French or Brugges hats in four years'.[2]

For a time the haberdasher was content to import his wares and sell

---

[2] Brewer, *Papers of Henry VIII*, No. 3107, Grants, 8 July, 1514, 27.

them for a modest profit to his rich customers. But eventually he began
to look closely at individual items and wonder whether it might not be
possible to have them made at home. Like the modern industrial pirate,
he would dismantle the cap, or glove, unpicking the stitches and
measuring its component parts so that it could be copied. Once he had
established a system for making the item it was an easy matter to find
cheap labour to manufacture it at a low price and thus increase his margin
of profit.

The haberdashers' greed for profit soon earned them the reputation of
exploiting the poor. This came to a head in 1517, on what became known
as Evil May Day, when a mob of London workmen and apprentices set
upon and killed a number of aliens. The workmen had been driven by
extreme desperation. The haberdashers, 'riche men', were accused of
flooding the market with imported goods, and reducing the living standards
of the craftsmen by forcing them to work for very low wages.

> Before May day pore peple percyved theym self having no lyvyng
> and wer bownd prentissis in London not able to kepe no howsis
> nor shops, but in allis sitting in a poore chamber working all the
> weke to sell his ware on the Saturday, brought it to the haburdashers
> to sell......which would not giff theym so moche wynning for their
> wares to fynde theym mete and drynk saying: they had no nede
> thereof; ther shopps lay storydd full of byond see.[3]

However, despite these grievances, the practice of haberdashers organising
subordinate crafts continued, and we find them operating in provincial
cities in much the same way as in London.

The first felt hats were imported from the continent by haberdashers.
They could not be made without fine foreign wool, so when feltmaking
began in Britain, the haberdashers also established themselves as importers
of wool from Spain and the East. They then sold it to the feltmakers in
small quantities at inflated prices, and brought back the finished product
at a very low price. Although the Haberdashers' Company swallowed
up the capping and hatting crafts, the feltmakers made it clear that they
were very unhappy with the situation. At heart they believed themselves
to be a company in their own right, although they had to admit that
they had 'no government of themselves as other companies have'.[4]
Feltmaking, although an infant craft, was growing rapidly. By 1576 there

---

[3] Quoted from Unwin, p. 82.
[4] Unwin, p. 131.

were 400 recorded native-born feltmakers in and around London. Soon afterwards, when they launched a campaign to obtain a royal charter, and consequently self-government, their leaders claimed to represent three thousand feltmakers.

These leaders, Bradford and Caunton, brought a case against merchants such as haberdashers, who, they claimed, were supplying feltmakers with sub-standard wool. Spanish, Estridge[5] and French wool was being brought into the country, 'unwashed and so full of May wool and other evil wool, dross, filthy dust and sand', that the feltmakers could not use a quarter of it.[6] The merchants tried to discredit their accusers by claiming that Bradford and Caunton were the 'worst sort of felters, haunters of taverns' who were exploiting 'poor men' and did not genuinely represent the three thousand feltmakers. Only partial victory was won, because the Lord Treasurer and Chief Justices ordered that, along with the master and warden of the haberdashers, five feltmakers would be appointed to inspect the foreign wool. This became a regular appointment with the feltmakers acting as assistants to the wardens of the haberdashers' company. But the feltmakers had other grievances which could not be satisfied by those with conflicting interests outside their own ranks. Their discontent culminated with a Bill to Parliament in 1601, and in 1604 they were granted a charter by James I. But even a royal charter could not liberate the feltmakers from the haberdashers, for they continued to act as merchants, importing wool and selling it on to the feltmakers.

Richard Bracebridge was not the first haberdasher to trade in Atherstone. Henry Blew, who died in 1534, left 'habberdashe & hosery' worth £44 out of a total wealth of only £50 4s. 2d.[7] The presence of a pack saddle amongst Blew's possessions might indicate a more itinerant business, whereby he fetched stocks of hosiery from merchants in Nottinghamshire or visited rich clients to sell them knitted silk stockings and embroidered caps. Blew was in business at the time when the haberdashers were well established as merchants trading in caps. He did not have far to travel to find a supply of goods, because Coventry, a major textile manufacturing centre in the medieval period, was still an important producer of felt caps

---

[5] Estridge wool came from eastern Europe and, like French wool, was coarse, though not as coarse as English wool which was rarely used in feltmaking. The finest wool came from Spain. See Bowden, p. 47, n. 3.

[6] Unwin, p. 132.

[7] Probate inventory, Lichfield Joint Record Office (hereafter L.J.R.O.) B/C/11, Henry Blew, 1523/4.

in the late sixteenth century, though by then the city's importance as a trading centre was on the decline.[8]

Richard's son, Samuel, born in 1612, was the first haberdasher of hats to be recorded in Atherstone.[9] It would have been natural for a man of his connection to have taken an apprenticeship in London but Samuel's name does not appear in the records of the Haberdashers or Feltmakers Companies. In 1634 Samuel married Susannah Moor, the daughter of John Moor of Shackerstone, Leicestershire. She bore him eleven children, all of whom were baptised at Mancetter Church, although only five survived to adulthood.

The years when Samuel and Susannah were raising their family were a time of great upheaval in England, when town and county factions were forced to ally themselves with the royalist or the parliamentarian cause. Significantly, the name of Bracebridge does not appear on any list of Warwickshire committeemen, sheriffs, justices or governors for the period 1645–60. We do not even know how their loyalties stood, although as men of commerce, it would be surprising if they were other than parliamentarian. It seems that Samuel Bracebridge spent the period of the civil war keeping out of trouble and concentrating on business.

By 1644 he was a copyholder with a croft and tenements in Atherstone, and over the following years he continued to accumulate copyhold land. He also had trading interests in Birmingham, where he owned a house and shop in High Street, worth £400. The overseers of the poor of Birmingham looked enviously on his growing wealth in Atherstone. He was liable for a tax of a mere forty shillings a year on the shop, so in 1652 they assessed him on all his Atherstone property, too. Samuel appealed to the county court which supported his case.[10] But Samuel obviously had strong connections with Birmingham because, after Susannah's death in 1661, he married Elizabeth Smallbrook there and took her to live in Atherstone. As a haberdasher of hats, Samuel was a merchant putting out wool to Atherstone cottagers, paying them for their labour and selling the finished 'country felts' on a wide market. There is no evidence that the Bracebridges ever actually made hats themselves.

The cottage feltmaker worked slowly on his hood in the spare moments between tending his crops and his livestock. It was also a time-consuming

---

[8] For a discussion of this decline see, C. Phythian-Adams, *Desolation of a City: Coventry and the Urban Crisis of the Late Middle Ages* (Cambridge, 1979).

[9] Bracebridge Family Papers, Copies of Pleadings, 1694, CR258/432, W.C.R.O.

[10] Ed. S. C. Ratcliff and H. C. Johnson, *Warwick County Records, Vol. III, Quarter Sessions Order Book, Easter 1650 to Epiphany 1657* (Warwick, 1937), p. 102.

business for the merchant, visiting the cottages, passing the time of day with the family, leaving a supply of wool, and collecting the few hats they would have completed in the week. Some weeks the more urgent demands of the land or the livestock would prevent them from completing the expected quota on time, and the merchant might be unable to hide his disappointment, even anger.

Samuel Bracebridge was not the only hatting entrepreneur in the parish. A large feltmaking shop had sprung up on the edge of Hartshill, a rural settlement, a mile or so from Atherstone. Samuel Butler was an unusual combination of gentleman and feltmaker. He had come from Alton in Hampshire to carry out the full range of hatting processes from feltmaking to trimming. His feltmaker's shop was situated close to a pond, which is just visible today at a road junction close to the Trent Valley railway line. Although excavation work has attempted to obliterate the features of the area, nature is not easily suppressed and the former mill pond still insists on showing itself as a reedy marsh. The spring which fed this pond provided Samuel Butler with the soft and pure water essential for his trade. He may have preferred to be in the town centre close to Watling Street, but the tanners of the town had appropriated all the waterside sites there. Butler's neighbours at Hartshill were also tanners, for Mill Lane is known today as Leather Mills Lane on account of two tanneries which took advantage of water from the River Anker which runs across it. Samuel Butler leased his premises from local squire, Edmund Parker, whose family had good trading credentials themselves. Formerly yeomen farmers, they had lived at Hartshill Castle for over a hundred years, first as tenants and later as owners. From the profits of their business as Merchant Grocers of the City of London, they were able to acquire more property around Hartshill.[11] One of these properties was Mill Lane Close, which Edmund Parker bought from John Vernon of Foxton in 1651.[12]

Why Samuel Butler came to Hartshill is not certain, although there is some evidence to suggest that he may have met Edmund Parker in Alton during the civil war.[13] Over succeeding generations the Butlers were amongst the most prosperous of Hampshire's merchant families.[14] Richard

[11] J. Allen, *Heardred's Hill: A History of Hartshill and Oldbury* (Nuneaton, 1982), p. 105.

[12] I am grateful to Joan Allen for this reference.

[13] G. N. Godwin, *The Civil War in Hampshire, 1642–45* (Southampton and London, 1904), p. 135, relates an anecdote which could provide an answer. In April 1644 an Edmund Parker was a prisoner of the Parliamentarians at Alton. If, by a slim chance, this is Edmund Parker of Hartshill, he may have met Samuel Butler there.

[14] D. Vick, *Lay Subsidy Assessment: 1558–1603, East Hampshire* (Hampshire, 1988).

Butler was a merchant, a water-bailiff's sergeant and keeper of the wool house in Southampton. He served as the City's mayor in 1551 and again in 1563 and 1564.[15] In Alton, a small clothmaking town, the Butlers were clothiers.[16] Feltmaking does not figure amongst the recorded manufactures of Alton, although it is likely that there were some feltmakers working there in the early seventeenth century. A second possibility is that Samuel was sent away to London to learn the craft, and there he is likely to have learned of the opportunities on offer in Warwickshire.

The early part of the seventeenth century was a time of cheap imports and the English feltmakers had to appeal to the monarch to help them in the fight to protect their industry. In 1623[17] and again in 1638[18] royal proclamations forbade the import of foreign caps and hats. The city guilds' restrictive practices added to the feltmakers' difficulties. On the other hand, the level of poverty in the countryside was rising, and people were desperate for work. It made good sense for Samuel Butler to move to an area where labour was cheap and he could get on with his work in freedom. He could also enjoy privacy, for his workshop was not in the centre of a settlement or even on a busy thoroughfare. Samuel Butler was established in Hartshill, living in the house he rented from Edmund Parker by the early 1650s. Two of the rooms were given up to feltmaking. In the 'cockloft', furnished with '4 tresles and 4 boards', men prepared and bowed the wool, then made the batts, which had to be carried carefully down from the loft on hurdles.[19] Butler had eight tod of wool in his workhouse. This was the equivalent of sixteen stone and would have been sufficient to make approximately 900 four-ounce hoods. With stocks as high as this, Butler posed a serious threat to Bracebridge, who had to rely on the fickle labour of the cottagers for putting out feltmaking.

In Butler's 'Workhouse', he had four basons, where the batt was initially worked gently to compress it before the laborious business of planking began. Butler had one 'walking plank' where up to eight men could be accommodated around the kettle. Three 'furnisses' provided the heat for the basoning, planking and stoving. The resulting hood would be blocked on a lime-wood hat block.[20] Blocking was hard work too, for the tight

---

[15] Ed. A. L. Merson, *The Third Book of Remembrance of Southampton, 1514–1602* (Southampton, 1955) Vol. I, p. 50; Vol. II, p. 154.

[16] W. M. Curtis, *History of Alton* (Winchester and London, 1896), p. 123.

[17] *Calendar of State Papers: Domestic – James I: Vol. CLII*, 17 Sept, 1623.

[18] *Calendar of State Papers: Domestic – Charles I: Vol. CCCXCI*, 26 May, 1638.

[19] Probate inventory, L.J.R.O. B/C/11, Samuel Butler, 1664. Transcribed by Joan Allen.

[20] Allen, p. 136.

dense felt would have to be pulled over the wooden block, requiring considerable strength and patience. In this period it was usual to dye hats after blocking, but Samuel Butler had no dye in his inventory, and neither was there a local dyer recorded for the period. But it was not essential to dye cheap country felts. They could be sold in their natural colour.

At least a dozen men were employed in Butler's feltmaking shop. The trimming would have been done at home by the wives and daughters of the feltmakers, who fixed a leather band inside the crown, and maybe a hatband outside the crown, too. When Butler died he left a stock of six and a half dozen hats, varying in value between £1 5s. 0d. and £2 0s. 0d. per dozen.

Butler's house was of moderate size; a hall, great chamber, store chamber, great parlour, little parlour, kitchen, brewhouse, buttery, cellar, cockloft, workhouse and yard. Although hatmaking was his prime business, he also had an interest in husbandry, and probably employed his feltmakers on the land when time and season allowed. In addition to a variety of farm animals, including twelve sheep, he had, '6 days work of winter corne & 6 days work of oates & peas' amounting to £14 14s. 4d. Like other inhabitants of Mancetter, Butler had cheese and bacon flitches, and brewed his own ale.

We do not know where Samuel Butler sold his wares, but as cheap country felts they could have been intended primarily for the provincial market, even if occasionally a few found their way to London by carrier. Although Butler and Bracebridge may have begun as competitors, it was not long before they were working together. Samuel Bracebridge, as a haberdasher of hats, would have bought some of Butler's produce, and may eventually have left him to organise all of the feltmaking. The two businesses would then have been complementary.

In 1656, the two men cemented their liaison on a more permanent basis. Samuel Bracebridge married off his eldest daughter, Susanna, aged twenty, to Butler's son, also Samuel. Whether Susanna had any say in the matter is not recorded, but the young couple appear to have moved away to Manchester, where they continued feltmaking and raised three children, Samuel, Sara and Susanna.[21]

Samuel Butler, Senior, had a daughter, Sarah, whom he married to one of his trading contacts from Coventry, Nathaniel Grascome, a clothier. When Samuel died in 1664, the lease on the Mill Lane house was left to

---

[21] Samuel Butler Junior, is recorded in the Bracebridge pedigree as, 'of Manchester, Co. Lancs.' See J. Nichols, *The History and Antiquities of the County of Leicester, Vol. III, Part II* (London, 1795, reprinted 1971), p. 1145.

his widow, but after her death in 1669 it passed to their son-in-law, Nathaniel. He farmed a little but does not appear to have engaged in any commercial activity. His interests were scholarly for his possessions included books and a desk. On his death, in 1670, he was recorded, not as a clothier, but as a 'clerk'.[22] Nathaniel appears to have died prematurely, for he left no will. Sarah had recently given birth to their fourth child and under the letters of administration had to enter into an agreement to 'Educate, foster and bringe up the said children with Sufficient and Convenyent Meate, Drink, Lodging and Apparell meete and decent for theire Estate.'[23] Sarah was also a Presbyterian, a member of a nonconformist sect which had in recent years been persecuted for non-attendance at the parish church. In 1675 she obtained a licence for a religious meeting at her home.[24]

It often happened that, when a master feltmaker died, his widow took over the business and continued to employ the journeymen. This was the only way in which a woman was officially allowed to work as a feltmaker. But in this case Samuel Butler's widow seems to have given up feltmaking altogether, for the trade was not carried on in Samuel Butler's workhouse after his death. Possibly it passed to the Bracebridges, for in 1664, Bracebridge's eldest son, Abraham, had completed his apprenticeship as a haberdasher of hats and was working with his father. Either Samuel Bracebridge moved the trade to Atherstone where it was absorbed into his own putting-out business, or Samuel Butler Junior took it up to Manchester, where feltmaking was already well established as a country craft. Whatever the case, the Butlers are not heard of again as feltmakers in the parish of Mancetter. They left the way clear for the Bracebridges, under whose control the business went from strength to strength.

---

[22] Probate inventory, L.J.R.O. B/C/11, Nathaniel Grascome, 1671.
[23] Bond of Sarah Grascome, L.J.R.O. B/C/11, Nathaniel Grascome, 1671.
[24] Allen, p. 129.

CHAPTER 4

Cottage Feltmakers
in the Seventeenth Century

IN THEIR QUEST for property and position, the Bracebridges left a wealth of deeds, indentures, wills and letters. Their letters, often written in the heat of the moment, show them to be moody, impatient and ruthless; unpleasant to their contemporaries, but fascinating subjects for the historian. Their marriage articles, penned on sheet after sheet of parchment, each the size of a table top, show a typical eighteenth-century pre-occupation with property and law. Their personalities, cheeseparing to the last farthing, come alive in the verbiage. We see demure, tight-bodiced girls with downcast eyes meekly standing by, whilst their fathers and prospective fathers-in-law hammer out a minor legal point before the bargain is struck.

If only a fraction of this attention could have been paid to their social inferiors, that huge sector of the population for whom there is little or no written record, other than that of their coming and going on this earth! Until this century, history scarcely concerned itself with such people. They had no vote, few rights and little property. Yet upon their labour the wealth of the merchant class was built.

What little we know of the cottagers and labourers has thus to be gleaned piece by piece from the fragmentary records which survive. They appear in manor rolls as occupiers of freehold or copyhold land. Occasionally they may even be listed as members of a jury, for often it was an advantage to the lord's steward to have a jury with which he could, 'Doe what he pleaseth'.[1] The parish register records their births, marriages and deaths, and the parish chest holds the documents which allow them to apply for poor relief. The quarter session records occasionally show them condemned to a flogging for petty theft, or fined for fathering a bastard child.

It is a painstaking task piecing together the few isolated facts which

---

[1] Records of Atherstone Manor, c. 1719, MR9, W.C.R.O.

survive, and fleshing them out to recreate a life. Probably the most fruitful quarry for gleaning facts about the poorer classes comes from the probate material. Although wills were usually left by the better off, who had goods and chattels to bequeath, a few of the poor did make wills and amongst them, the occasional artisan. The poor are also named on the wills and inventories of the better off, as appraisers, beneficiaries and witnesses.

An inventory of the deceased person's possessions was drawn up by two or three neighbours, soon after death. They went through the house from room to room, listing everything, and then out into the yard to the barns, and even the fields to appraise the crops. More than any other document, the inventory allows us to form a picture of a person's day-to-day life; the activities carried on in the different rooms of the house. We can visualise the household goods in use for cooking, cheese-making, spinning and brewing. From the wills we can build up kinship networks and business contacts. We can see which relatives were in favour with the deceased and which were out of favour. Family frictions and black sheep are there by implication and omission.[2]

So how did the humble cottagers earn their living in the seventeenth century, before enclosure took away their livelihood? Many paid rent of a few pence per week to the lord of the manor for a modest cottage in the town. A few paid rent to a freeholder, or even a copyholder, who had more than one holding and could reap the financial benefits of letting vacant property. Having no strips of their own in the three open fields which surrounded the town, the cottagers could earn money and beer by labouring for the better off. Work was plentiful for all the family, from muck trenching in winter to weeding the crops in spring, then reaping the harvest in late summer, and threshing the grain. After harvest the cottagers were allowed to gather the gleanings, and some would even travel to other manors to follow the harvest.

They had generous rights of common. Fireboot gave them the right to take wood from the commons, which they could use themselves or sell to the better off. Those who could afford a beast, or a horse, had the right to graze the open fields at the appropriate season. A horse was a valuable asset. With a cart it could be used to fetch coals from the coalfields which outcropped on the hillside approaching the Arden. The coal could then be sold to the townsfolk. A horse and cart could also be hired out

[2] Inventories and wills for the Parish of Mancetter are held at Lichfield Joint Record Office, and are currently being transcribed by Atherstone Local History Research Group.

to transport goods further afield, or a family to their new parish of settlement.[3]

At home, even before feltmaking came into the rural economy, there was a small cottage industry. Wool and flax are found in the sixteenth and seventeenth century inventories. Carding and spinning provided occupation for women, whilst men did weaving. By the standards of many rural communities the cottagers of Atherstone were well off. Generous rights of common gave them a certain independence. It was said during the battle against enclosure, the following century, that under the open field system a landless cottager could adjust his labour to provide the livelihood his family required. When extra money was needed for an occasional expense such as a daughter's dowry, there was scope to increase one's labour to meet the need. The cottagers had the flexibility to earn their bread by a variety of means as the seasons dictated. They were beholden to no man but their landlord for rent, and the lord of the manor for his quarterly dues. And those who paid less than twenty shillings a year in rent were exempt from the hearth tax when it was introduced in 1662. It seems fairly clear that these advantages drew people in large numbers to this Warwickshire town, ensuring that the houses were always occupied. The pressure for housing would later result in the fragmentation of burgages, eventually degenerating into the overcrowded yard system of the nineteenth century.

In the year 1655, Samuel Butler had established his feltmaking shop in Hartshill and Samuel Bracebridge was working as a haberdasher of hats. Both offered the possibility of employment and, as a result, young people were being drawn into the trade. 1655 is the first of three years in Cromwell's commonwealth period when persons marrying were required to furnish details of occupation for the parish register. In 1655 there were more marriages recorded in Mancetter Church than in any other year of the century. Five out of the twenty-one marriages were of feltmakers. All but one of these couples were to stay in the parish working as feltmakers and raising children who would also enter the trade. These children would be wealthy enough to leave modest wills and inventories, showing that once feltmaking was established in a family, it was likely to persist.

The short period between 1655 and 1657 stands out so clearly from the records that it is tempting to see it as a period of particular prosperity when young feltmakers were more financially secure than at any other time, perhaps because of the employment opportunities offered by

---

[3] Bracebridge Papers: Papers of Grievances, c. 1730, HR35/10, W.C.R.O.

Bracebridge and Butler. However, it may well have been that other periods were equally rich in feltmaker marriages, but the details are not recorded. Although there was a high marriage rate during this period, it did not lead to a high rate of baptism amongst the feltmakers. In fact, 1655 marked the beginning of a sharp fall in the baptism over burial figures, and this fall continued for the next four years, indicating perhaps a visitation of the plague, a horror which recurred at regular intervals throughout the century. But, however virulent the epidemic, it did not prevent the young feltmakers from surviving and producing children, some of whom were wealthy enough to leave probate documents, although in most cases their assets were modest.

In addition to the subjects of the wills and inventories, the names of the witnesses and beneficiaries can tell us something about the relationship of the cottagers to their social superiors. Alongside his elaborate inventory, the will of Samuel's son, Abraham Bracebridge, of 1692, itemises the following, 'I give & bequeth unto John Martin the best of my wearring apparrell and to Abraham Muston the worst to be divided by my executrix'.[4] John Martin, also a witness to the will, acknowledges his legacy, describing himself as a 'Feltmaker'.[5] Martin was obviously Bracebridge's right-hand man. One can imagine Abraham Bracebridge sitting in his study, with his executor and brother-in-law, Thomas Charnells, penning the last lines of his will. He summons Martin and two other servants from their work. They approach, fearful of his purpose, heads bent in submission. Charnells signs first in a confident and scholarly flourish. Then it is John Martin's turn. With a slow and shaky hand he is just able to inscribe the initials, 'I.M.', before an impatient clerk pushes him away and adds the explanation, 'His marke'.

Though Martin and Muston were termed 'servants', they did not live within the curtilage of Abraham's home, Atherstone Hall. The Hall was very close to the cottages of the town, where these men lived modestly, and from whence they could conveniently be at the beck and call of their master. Bracebridge's inventory, unlike Samuel Butler's, does not list a workshop or any feltmaking equipment, merely stock. John Martin, having been described as a feltmaker, was likely to be practising his craft, and if there was no felt shop at Atherstone Hall, he would have been working at home.

Another cottage feltmaker was Joseph Hatton, born in 1658, the son

---

[4] Will of Abraham Bracebridge, 1692, CR258/229, W.C.R.O.
[5] Probate documents, John Martin, 1695, MR9/80, W.C.R.O.

of Nicholas Hatton, also a feltmaker who married in 1657, the last year for which we have a detailed parish register. He is the poorest of the feltmakers to leave inventories. Aged thirty-eight when he died, he occupied a two-room cottage, comprising a 'dwelling house' and a 'workhouse'. His few possessions included, '2 poore old kettles & 3 Sorry Basons and Hattblocks & other old lumber', valued at 9s. 4d.[6] The fact that no stock of hats or wool is listed suggests that he, too, was one of Bracebridge's cottage feltmakers. This was to be a family tradition, for in 1740 his son would be described by Abraham Bracebridge II as, 'My old Servant, Joseph Hatton'.[7] Like John Martin and Abraham Muston in the previous generation, Joseph was to be a beneficiary under Abraham Bracebridge's will, and to receive his 'wearing Apparell'. Clothes were expensive possessions, often the most valuable items in a person's will. It is a mark of Bracebridge's gratitude for his faithful service that he bequeathed his clothes to Joseph.

How satisfying it would be to be able to construct a hierarchy of the local hatting trade; to identify those who were working as master feltmakers and those who were journeymen. But, because feltmaking migrated to these country districts to escape the restrictions of the guilds, very few of these men would have completed formal apprenticeships. Indeed, on the rare occasions when the word, 'apprentice' is used we do not know how stringently the term was applied to the young man's position. The London feltmakers regarded country journeymen as unskilled and forbade them to be employed unless it was for making 'course Felt hats'.[8] Some began apprenticeships in London, then applied for their freedom to 'go into the Country'.[9] Presumably, they had learned enough of the craft under a qualified master to allow them to get by in the country. No doubt there were also times when family hardships, such as the death of a father, caused them to break their apprenticeship to return home and become the breadwinner. How reluctantly the young apprentice would have left his master's house in the City of London, to travel the long journey home, away from his new and sophisticated friends, with their talk of foreign countries and fashionable patrons.

A young apprentice, John Walmsley, had to leave his London master, Richard Hiles, before his term was complete. In 1693 he paid a ten shilling severance fine to obtain his freedom, and a certificate which

---

[6] Probate inventory, L.J.R.O. B/C/11, Joseph Hatton, 1696.
[7] Will of Abraham Bracebridge, 1740, CR258/239, W.C.R.O.
[8] Feltmakers' Court Minute Book, September 1695, Guildhall Library, Ms 1570/2.
[9] Feltmakers' Court Minute Book, January 1693 and May 1693, GL Ms 1570/2.

allowed him to go into the country to help his father, John Walmsley, in Atherstone.[10]

Thomas Wilday, himself a feltmaker, sent his son, Samuel, away to London at the age of seventeen to learn the trade. He was bound apprentice in 1682 for eight years to Richard Thomas, a master feltmaker and member of the Livery Company.[11] His 'quarteridge', or wages, amounted to one shilling, and, as the word implies, was paid every quarter by his master. The five shilling fee necessary to bind him apprentice would have been paid by Samuel's father, unless he had a wealthy sponsor. In later years the Wildays were to work for the Bracebridges, and it could have been that Samuel Wilday was sponsored by Abraham Bracebridge. But if that were the case, why did Bracebridge not give his own son the benefit of a London apprenticeship?

Sometimes Atherstone feltmakers moved away to work elsewhere. Thomas Hartell married Elizabeth Shaw, the daughter of a glazier in the City of Coventry. Four years after their marriage at Mancetter Church, the couple settled in Coventry and Thomas was recorded in the Cappers' Company account book for 1659, when he submitted his proof piece for admission as a journeyman.[12] He was then aged thirty, and as a country feltmaker he would have had to work hard to satisfy the Cappers and Feltmakers that he was worthy of joining their prestigious fellowship.[13]

Occasionally feltmakers migrated to Atherstone. Thomas's sister, Ester, married William Pickford, who came from elsewhere to work as a feltmaker. He may have been introduced to Ester by Thomas. Richard Hanson of Tamworth married Elizabeth, the daughter of Alice Abell, a widow. Alice Abell had married into a wealthy tanning and shoemaking family, but was reported to be in 'desperate arrears' with her hearth tax in 1663, by which time her daughter and son-in-law were living and working in Market Street, Tamworth.[14]

Poverty was a frequent visitor to the cottagers, whose subsistence level could so easily fall under a bad harvest. In 1654 there had been a plea to

---

[10] Feltmakers' Court Minute Book, January 1693, GL Ms 1570/2.

[11] Feltmakers' Court Minute Book, May 1682, GL Ms 1570/1.

[12] Account Book of the Fellowship of Cappers in the City of Coventry, 1659, 1494/20/1, Coventry City Record Office.

[13] Although, since medieval times, Coventry had been an important producer of felt caps, when feltmaking became established, the Cappers took feltmaking under their jurisdiction too. By 1639 they had changed their name to the 'Company and Fellowship of Cappers and Feltmakers in the City of Coventry'.

[14] Ed. M. Walker, *Warwick County Records: Hearth Tax Returns, Vol. I, Hemlingford Hundred: Tamworth and Atherstone Divisions* (Warwick, 1957), pp. 41, 252.

the county court from the inhabitants of Atherstone to force other townships in the parish to share in the relief of the 'great number of their poor'.[15] Poverty then, as now, could lead a person towards crime. The records for Southwark, where the early immigrants settled, are scattered with transgressing feltmakers, whose crimes range from deviant sexual practices involving animals, to theft and murder. The comparatively small number of feltmakers living around Atherstone does not allow for the same level of crime. Furthermore, the county sheriff's bailiffs, responsible for the town, were often feltmakers themselves and may have been lenient towards their fellow craftsmen. Indeed some of the Levelling philosophies of the revolution might well have filtered through to them, and were put into practice when the opportunity arose.

Sheriff's bailiffs, and feltmakers, William Musson and Thomas Wilday, were in trouble in 1674 for illegally extorting six shillings from William Purefoy of Caldecote Hall, nephew of Colonel Purefoy, the regicide.[16] Two years later Thomas Wilday was in trouble again, this time for falsely imprisoning one of his fellow townsmen.[17] Shakespeare's character, Dull, the constable in *Love's Labours Lost,* brings to life the self-important parish officer, whose intelligence is not a match for his ego. It was a dubious honour to be selected for authority over one's peers and isolated the individual within the community.

But, despite any abuse of power, Thomas Wilday remained a man of modest means. When he died in 1687, he left a total wealth of £8 10s. 6d,. including, 'in the Shop some hatt blocks 2 basins and some old Workinge geare', valued at 10s. 2d.[18] He is entered in the hearth tax returns as either 'Non Liable' or 'exempt' from payment on his single hearth. Like Joseph Hatton's, Thomas Wilday's inventory lists no stock, suggesting that he, too, was in the employ of the Bracebridges. It is probably no coincidence that Bracebridge's men were selected as sheriff's bailiff, for Abraham Bracebridge himself was to become sheriff for Warwickshire in 1694.

Another transgressing feltmaker was Samuel Fox, whose mother, Katherine, was one of the more prosperous feltmaker widows, carrying on the business after her husband's death. Samuel was indicted at the Michaelmas

[15] Ed. S. C. Ratcliff and H. C. Johnson, *Warwick County Records: Vol.III, Quarter Sessions Order Book, Easter 1650 to Epiphany 1657* (Warwick, 1941), p. 201.

[16] Ratcliff and Johnson, *Vol. VI Quarter Sessions, Easter 1631 to Epiphany 1674* (Warwick, 1941), p. 201.

[17] Ratcliff and Johnson, *Vol. VII Quarter Sessions, Easter 1674 to Easter 1682* (Warwick, 1946), p. 63.

[18] Probate inventory, L.J.R.O. B/C/11, Thomas Wilday, 1687.

Quarter Sessions of 1684 for stealing six hats, worth eleven pence, from Thomas Orne. In common with other feltmakers, Fox was described as a 'labourer', alluding both to the seasonal nature of the work, and also to the lowly status of feltmaking. He confessed to the misdeed but did not escape a flogging at Atherstone.[19]

Apart from the poor cottage feltmakers, who were either recipients of the Bracebridge putting-out system, or employed in Butler's felt shop, there was a middling group of feltmakers. Little is known about them, but they appear to be independent and would later become gentrified, leaving the trade for a higher social calling. The Foxes and the Walmsleys come into this category. Both families were long established in the area and had intermarried.

The Walmsleys first appear in the Mancetter parish records in 1592. They were probably involved in headwear making at an early date, for in 1605 one of them is recorded as paying 'Chappell rente' to the Cappers' Company in Coventry.[20] In 1663, a later member, John Walmsley, had a house with five hearths, making him one of Atherstone's more affluent residents. His son, John, was to acquire substantial property in the town, and become bailiff of the manor. His independence from the Bracebridges was evident in 1692 when Samuel Bracebridge died. He exacted a second heriot from Samuel's son, Abraham. A mere cottage feltmaker would not have dared to oppose his master in this way.

John's cousin, Thomas, had a very different lifestyle. In 1671 he is described as 'very poore' and only able to manage a part payment of his hearth tax.[21] He was probably one of Bracebridge's cottage feltmakers, and passed on the trade to his children. When his son's widow, Anne, died in 1690, she bequeathed her feltmaking equipment to her children. This consisted of, 'in the Shopp two old Working kettles & 2 basons of Iron Mettle 3 bowes & 3 hurdles 2 duzen of old hatt blocks'. The fact that no stock is listed suggests that her husband, too, had been working for Bracebridge.[22]

The hearth tax was introduced by Charles II after his Restoration to help replenish the empty treasury coffers, for bankruptcy had been one of the reasons why the Protectorate failed. It is a useful indicator of living standards, but it has not yet been proven beyond doubt that feltmakers'

---

[19] Ratcliff and Johnson, *Vol. VIII Quarter Sessions, Trinity 1682 to Epiphany 1690* (Warwick, 1953), p. 104.

[20] Account Book of the Fellowship of Cappers, 1605, 1494/20/1, Coventry City Record Office.

[21] Ed. Walker, *Hearth Tax Returns, Vol. I*, p. 258.

[22] Probate inventory, L.J.R.O. B/C/11, Anne Walmsley, 1690.

hearths, like those of bakers and blacksmiths, were exempt from the tax. Often it depended upon the local official's interpretation of the rules. 'Non-liable' on a feltmaker's hearth could mean that the hearth was classed as industrial, or that the feltmaker was too poor to pay. As feltmakers were almost always the poorer members of the community, it is virtually impossible to discriminate between the two categories.

John Walmsley's sister, Katherine, was married to John Fox, another feltmaker. Katherine and John settled in Mancetter in 1635. They raised a large family and like most cottage feltmakers, they appear to have had a relatively poor standard of living. John died in 1658, leaving his widow to continue making hats. At her death in 1682 she had built up a reasonable business, with a stock of wool, hats and trimming materials in a total wealth of £42 4s. 4d., putting Katherine amongst the more affluent of Mancetter's seventeenth century deceased.[23] She may have been working on her own account, for in country areas it was not unknown for women to work in the plank shops.[24] As mentioned earlier, women could not be bound apprentice to feltmakers and become journeymen or masters, but widows were allowed to take over their dead husband's trade and could, under those circumstances, bind apprentices in their own name.[25] Katherine Fox may also have been engaged in hat trimming, the part of the trade traditionally done by women. 'In the hall' she had:

> One smoothing iron 2 heaters one paire of bellowes nine & twenty hatts one dozen of hat linings one dozen of hatbands one looking glass 2 hatcases & other od bands appraised at £3 16s. 4d.[26]

The inclusion of a looking glass suggests that she was running a retail business, with clients coming to her house to have hats trimmed to their particular requirements. Retail business was very common in the later centuries, when account books record the names of individual customers. Katherine's inventory contains no feltmaking equipment, although in her will she bequeaths to her eldest surviving son, Samuel, 'all [her] workinge tooles belonginge to the trade of a hatter.'[27] It seems that this bequest

---

[23] Probate inventory, L.J.R.O. B/C/11, Katherine Fox, 1682.

[24] J. H. Smith, p. 85

[25] See Phythian-Adams, p. 91. Also the Feltmakers' Court Book, Guildhall Library, which gives examples of women taking apprentices, often their own sons, e.g. 'Sept 1697, William Burton, son of William Burton, late Citizen and Feltmaker deceased, bound to Dorcas his mother, Relict of the Said William Burton deceased, for 7 years.' GL Ms 1570/2.

[26] Probate inventory, L.J.R.O. B/C/11, Katherine Fox, 1682.

[27] Will, L.J.R.O. B/C/11, Katherine Fox, 1682.

did not prevent Samuel from slipping into crime, but his mother did not live to witness the shame of her son's public flogging in the market place.

In the 'Chamber over the Hall', Katherine had:

> One pack of Welshe Woole 3 Todd & six and sixe pound more of Welsh Woole one Tod and twenty six pounds of Lambs woole and foure pound and a halfe of od woole appraised at £12 17s. 6d.

No other Mancetter inventory includes Welsh wool, of which one breed was the only British wool to be fine enough for feltmaking. This sheep, the Ryeland, had a small fine fleece, with fibres said to be only $\frac{1}{750}$ inch in diameter.[28] It was bred in Archenfield near Monmouth, on the Welsh border, and was known as the 'Golden Fleece of Leominster' on account of its felting qualities.

The inventories, wills and parish registers can tell us a little about feltmaking in Mancetter in the seventeenth century, but it is probably fair to say that the evidence available indicates only a fraction of the activity. There was an extensive local trade which has left very little documentary evidence. Most regrettable is the lack of any indication of market outlets. Who bought the hats? Where did they go? We know that in later years they equipped armies, but in the seventeenth century, with wide and floppy brims, Atherstone hats were more likely to be found on the heads of peasants. Indeed, the feltmakers' own peer group were the most likely wearers.

When enclosure was first mooted in 1730, cottage feltmaking was a major part of the local economy. Objections were raised against enclosing the commons because, 'Many Tradesmen of a lower Rank' depended upon the grazing for keeping a horse, 'In a dull time of Trade', when they would undertake carting or hiring. This was the case for the 'Two most considerable Manufactures in the said Town, Tammy weaving and Feltmaking'.[29]

Hatting, as a cottage industry, involved the whole family and was an example of the classic proto-industrial domestic system. Like other areas of the textile industry, certain tasks were performed by certain members of the family. Women and children would sort, clean and card the wool, which the men would bow and form into batts. The felt would be made at a kettle over the hearth, and the resulting hood could also be shaped, then trimmed by the women. The finished hat would be collected by

---

[28] K. Buckland, 'The Monmouth Cap', reprinted from *Costume*, Vol. 13 (1979), p. 10.

[29] Bracebridge Papers: Paper of Grievances, c.1736, HR35/10, W.C.R.O.

Bracebridge's men, who paid the family per piece. Not all families would finish the hat. It could be collected at the hood stage, then sent elsewhere for trimming, or sold in its unfinished state. Indeed, as a country felt, it would probably have remained undyed and required very little trimming.

There are no contemporary descriptions of cottage feltmaking. But Daniel Defoe's description of the Yorkshire cloth industry in 1724 conveys a little of the atmosphere of domestic trade in general:

> Among the manufacturers' houses are likewise scattered an infinite number of cottages or small dwellings, in which dwell the workmen which are employed, the women and children of whom, are always busy carding, spinning &c. so that no hands being unemployed, all can gain their bread, even from the youngest to the ancient; hardly any thing above four years old, but its hands are sufficient to it self.
>
> This is the reason also why we saw so few people without doors; but if we knocked at the door of any of the master manufacturers, we presently saw a house full of lusty fellows, some at the dye-fat, some dressing the cloths, some in the loom, some one thing, some another, all hard at work, and full employed upon the manufacture, and all seeming to have sufficient business.[30]

For the 'lusty weaver' we must substitute the feltmaker, half-naked and sweating over his steaming kettle. Perhaps he was a little rougher than his northern brother, and a little more inclined towards his beer. But in the seventeenth century he had space around him; a garden to grow vegetables and as much summer work in the open fields as his family could wish. Within a hundred years, enclosure would bring a loss of independence, and the first steps towards an industrial economy, where husbandry would no longer have a part to play.

---

[30] D. Defoe, *A Tour Through the Whole Island of Great Britain,* First published 1724–26 (Penguin reprint 1971), p. 493.

CHAPTER 5

Abraham Bracebridge I:
The Fight Over His Father's Will

THE FIRST Abraham Bracebridge was born in Atherstone in 1642, the year in which civil war broke out. It appears that, unlike the earlier watershed of 1485, this momentous event of English history passed Atherstone by. At Caldecote Hall, three miles away, William Purefoy had taken up arms against King Charles I, and was later to become one of the signatories of his death warrant. But, whilst history was being made by their neighbours, the people of Atherstone seem to have taken little part in the war. The burial of a soldier who came 'sick to this town' is one of only a few minor events recorded in the parish records.[1] Perhaps this is surprising for a town which lay on one of the country's main thoroughfares, and it may be that when more work has been done on the impact of the civil war in north Warwickshire, a different picture will emerge.

Abraham was Samuel Bracebridge's eldest son. He served an apprenticeship as a haberdasher of hats before joining his father in the Atherstone trade, and at the age of thirty became engaged to Mary Charnells of nearby Snarestone in Leicestershire. Samuel, now a widower, was in his sixties and beginning to feel the weight of his years. He believed that he no longer wanted the full responsibility of business. But rather than pass on the trade to his rightful heir, his eldest son, he sold it to him. Furthermore, the old man drove a hard bargain, and Abraham was made to pay £1000, in instalments over four years. It was a high price, 'More than the stock [was] worth,' he said later.[2] However, it could well be said that this was a diplomatic move by Samuel, to prevent any sibling jealousy, or accusation of favouritism towards his eldest son, for he had in fact

---

[1] Mancetter Parish Register: Burials, 14 June 1649, DR130/1, W.C.R.O.

[2] This and other references to the dispute between Abraham Bracebridge and his two brothers, are contained in the Bracebridge family papers: Abraham Bracebridge and Martha Blore *v.* Shem Bracebridge *et al.*, 1694, CR258/431, W.C.R.O.

given Abraham the wherewithal to purchase the business in the form of a settlement on his marriage of at least £1000.

In 1672, Abraham took over as master of the business and the family home, an imposing residence with eleven hearths, the third largest in the town. His brothers and sisters had all left home, though Martha, married to the vicar of Mancetter, William Blore, was living locally and would remain her brother's close ally throughout his future troubles. Abraham's eldest sister, Susanna, who had married Samuel Butler Junior and moved to Manchester, had died in 1669, leaving three children. His younger brother, Thomas, had been appointed vicar of Ab Kettleby in Leicestershire by his father, who purchased the advowson for that purpose. Thomas was married to Jane Ludford, heiress to the coal-rich estate of Ansley in the neighbouring parish. Abraham's youngest brother, Shem, had also served an apprenticeship as a haberdasher of hats, and afterwards his father had given him £500 to set up in business with a Mr Sumers. Subsequently Shem was enrolled as a member of the Mercers' Company and settled in the City of London as a merchant. He remained unmarried, and once or twice a year paid brief visits to Atherstone, to spend a day or two with his father.

Whilst Samuel remained living nearby with his second wife, Elizabeth Smallbrook, Abraham and Mary settled down to life and business in Atherstone. The relationship between father and son was often strained, because although in theory Samuel had handed over the reins to Abraham, in practice he could not resist interfering. In April 1676, after Elizabeth died, it appears that Samuel made his will. There was generous provision for all his children, and his grandchildren, Samuel, Sara and Susanna Butler. Between them, Samuel spread his considerable wealth. Thomas was to have an estate at Ibstock, and Shem an estate at Swepston, plus a derelict inn on a valuable site in Birmingham. Martha was to be given land at Stretton, and Susanna's children were to have legacies for investment until they came of age.

Having written his will, Samuel went on, over the next nine years, to settle more money and property on his children. Like King Lear, he gradually gave all away, but expected his family to love and care for him until he died. Whether they did or not, remains a matter for debate. When he was seventy-five, Samuel suffered a stroke, a 'paralytic distemper', which affected his brain. However, from time to time he rallied, and in his more lucid moments, with the help of servants, he was able to manage the accounts. One can imagine Abraham sitting in his study, poring over the ledgers. His father would walk in unannounced, and Abraham would be forced to suppress his annoyance when Samuel looked over his shoulder to see the latest entry. Even worse, he would open up other books and question Abraham on certain entries, occasionally demanding to see the receipts. Abraham had to humour his father, lest he fly into a tantrum and demand to see his lawyers for a redraft of his will.

In 1688 Samuel realised that he was not long for this world, and made

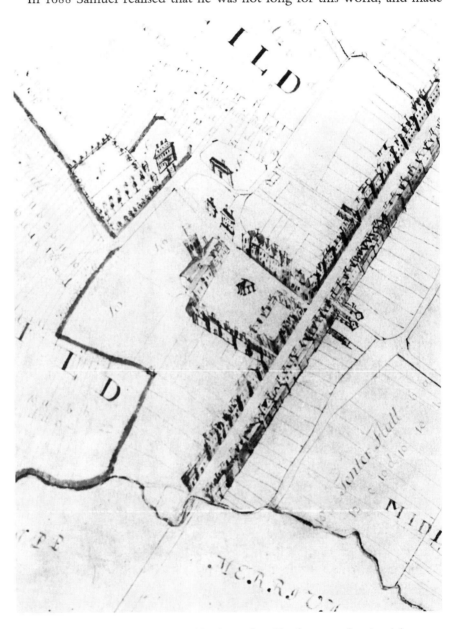

7. Detail of 'A Plan of Atherston Feildes' by Robert Hewitt, 1716, showing Atherstone town centre with Atherstone Hall, in its grounds, towards the top left of the picture.

some hasty preparations for his arrival in the next. He set up a trust to pay £10 a year for a minister to read prayers in Atherstone chapel on alternate Sundays, saving people the walk to Mancetter church, which could be unpleasant in bad weather, especially for the elderly and very young. He also allocated twenty shillings a year for a schoolmaster or mistress to teach the children of the poor.

Meanwhile, Abraham, through astute management of the hatting business, had become sufficiently prosperous to buy Atherstone Hall from the lord of the manor, Seabright Repington, whose family had lived there only briefly, preferring their seat at Amington near Tamworth. Not satisfied with the 'fair house of Brick' which John Repington had built in 1619 on the site of an Augustinian friary, Abraham set about rebuilding in the fashion of the day. Although no plans are extant, a field map of 1716, which shows buildings in perspective, gives an indication that the style he chose was characteristic of a newly rich businessman with protestant loyalties.[3]

The two-storey house was built in the solid but elegant style of Sir Christopher Wren's country houses, with a hipped roof and dormer windows. The roof space accommodated three garret rooms and a cheese chamber, which appears to have been used as a bedroom. His trade of putting out wool to be made up by the cottagers was, like their own occupation, part of the domestic household. Abraham had his study on the ground floor, close to the hat chamber, and the men who worked for him, John Martin and Abraham Muston, lived in nearby cottages.[4]

In October 1692, aged eighty, Samuel died. His life had spanned five reigns, from the Stuart King James I, through the turmoil of the civil war and the execution of Charles I, followed by Cromwell's eleven-year commonwealth, the restoration of the monarchy in 1660, the Jacobite risings and finally, the Glorious Revolution of 1689.

Samuel's funeral in Mancetter brought his family together for a last time, although Shem remained in London. Perhaps, with hindsight, he should have made the effort to attend, for a few days later he received a letter from Abraham, asking whether letters of administration should be taken out in London or in the country. Shem was surprised. Why were letters of administration needed? Father had made a will. He had often talked about it, making his wishes known to the family.

No, Abraham told him, there was no will. He had searched through

---

[3] A Plan of Atherston Feildes, Robert Hewitt, 1716, P7, W.C.R.O.
[4] Inventory of Abraham Bracebridge, 1694, CR258/261, W.C.R.O.

his papers, but there was no will to be found, anywhere. Samuel had died intestate. Shem had no reason to disbelieve his brother, and agreed that letters of administration should be taken out at the Prerogative Court of Canterbury, as befitted his wealth, and the fact that he owned property in more than one diocese. An inventory was prepared by Samuel's 'indifferent' neighbours. These were John Allsop, Richard Goodwin, and Samuel Power, all tradesmen who lived nearby in the market place, in houses they rented from Bracebridge.[5]

By now Shem had discussed the matter with his brother, Thomas, the vicar of Ab Kettleby, and the two of them were beginning to have second thoughts about Abraham's honesty. They became convinced that he had persuaded the appraisers to understate their father's wealth. They wondered why there were no jewels or plate recorded on the inventory, except a tankard, four old spoons, a thimble and a little chain to hang a cross on.[6]

The tankard was already the subject of a dispute with the lord of the manor over a claim for heriot. After Samuel's death the lord of the manor's bailiff, John Walmsley, former feltmaker and nephew of Katherine Fox, visited the house and demanded two fine horses in respect of the two houses which Samuel held by copyhold from the manor. Abraham refused to hand over the horses, and subsequently one of the horses was sold for £4 10s. 0d. Soon afterwards John Walmsley returned to the house with a second bailiff, Samuel Grew, and asked for this money. Bracebridge laid eighteen five shilling pieces on the table which Walmsley picked up and pocketed. He then asked to see the silver tankard which had been listed on the inventory.[7] This was brought at once and Walmsley lifted it up and examined it, remarking that it was a fine cup, and he would like to see how well ale tasted from it. Ale was brought and the bailiff drank it down quickly. He then put the cup into his pocket and walked out, saying that his lordship would be pleased with it. It was said of the money and the tankard, that Walmsley and Grew, had 'converted them to their own use', and indeed, when John Walmsley died in 1712, he left amongst his possessions, a silver tankard.[8] Could it be that the lord of the manor never received his heriot?

Abraham Bracebridge would not be ridden roughshod over, and with

[5] Inventory of Samuel Bracebridge, 1692, CR258/429, W.C.R.O.

[6] Bracebridge papers: Abraham Bracebridge and Martha Blore *v.* Shem Bracebridge *et al.*, 1694, CR258/432, W.C.R.O.

[7] Miscellaneous documents relating to the manor of Atherstone, c.1692, MR9/37, W.C.R.O.

[8] Will of John Walmsley, 1712, CR258/259, W.C.R.O.

the support of Atherstone's more prominent copyholders, some of whom had been engaged in similar disputes with the Repingtons, he began a legal action against the lord for breaching manorial custom. Although the Assizes found in Abraham's favour, he recovered only £3 plus costs of £10, whereas his own legal costs had amounted to £26.[9] But the point had been made. The absentee lord was forced to sack his steward, Francis Gramer, tighten up the system, and put right a long list of breaches of custom.

Within weeks Abraham was embroiled in a legal battle with his family. Only Martha accepted that Samuel had died intestate. The others insisted on finding out exactly what had happened to their father's will. Abraham had a ready answer. He remembered his father making some notes, which seemed to be for a will, but it was a long time ago and he could not remember the details. It wasn't important, for why did Samuel need a will? He had made generous provision for his children. Martha had been given the estate in Stretton, surely that was enough for her? Mr Mounteney, Samuel's solicitor, had other ideas. 'He did intend to make a will,' he said. It had been about seven years ago, and he distinctly remembered being summoned for the very purpose of taking instructions to draw up a will. He had settled with Samuel in his study and was just about to start when company entered and the will had to be forgotten. Abraham was not quite of the same mind. He insisted that he had often heard his father say, on the subject of wills, that he had made none and nor would he make any!

Abraham's story did not convince his brothers, Thomas and Shem, or his grandchildren, who took the matter to the High Court. Abraham was quite adamant that his father had already made generous provision for all his family, and that the residue was intended for him, as the eldest son. He believed that he deserved it, because for many years before illness disabled him, Samuel had lost interest in business matters, and had depended on Abraham to invest his capital wisely. Abraham was proud that he had increased the value of his father's estate. Thomas and Shem had chosen to leave home and had made lives for themselves elsewhere. Whereas, Abraham, as a dutiful eldest son, had stayed with his father, caring for him, and looking after the business. He believed that he deserved to inherit his father's estate. Samuel's books, which he had carefully kept up-to-date were there for all to see. He had drawn up the accounts until Samuel's

---

[9] Bracebridge papers: Abraham Bracebridge and Martha Blore *v.* Shem Bracebridge *et al.*, 1694, CR258/432, W.C.R.O.

death, and annexed them to his plea. The balance was there before them, a precise, two hundred and seventy four pounds, three shillings and eight pence three farthings. It was all laid out in the schedules for the plaintiff's 'better satisfaction', but none of them had ever asked to see it.[10]

It was natural that Samuel should appreciate the care and support of his eldest son and the devotion of his younger daughter, Martha. She understood that her father had made a will and that it had been destroyed, but how or when, she could not say. All she hoped was that she could obtain from the estate what was hers by right.

In December 1693, at the age of fifty, Abraham became seriously ill. His brothers were worried that he would die before the case was settled. They hoped that he might live a year, not because they had any brotherly affection for him, but because they wanted to lay claim to their father's estate. Their wishes were not fulfilled, for although Abraham appears to have survived until February 1695, the matter was not settled before his death. It was left to his widow, Mary, as executrix to take up the case in July 1696 and the matter was still in court in May 1697.

Abraham had made his own will in July 1692, four months before Samuel's death.[11] It shows him as having built up a substantial estate, with lands in several Warwickshire and Leicestershire parishes, including the manor of Lindley, a short distance from Mancetter. This house was to come into the possession of Abraham's eldest son, Samuel. He had studied law at Brasenose College, Oxford, was a member of the Inner Temple, and in 1710 he would be elected as member of parliament for Tamworth.

Abraham's second son, Thomas, was still serving an apprenticeship as a haberdasher of hats. He was left land at Hartshill, near Samuel Butler's former feltshop. Samuel Butler's son had stayed in Manchester after his father's death, when the lease on the house in Hartshill had passed to Butler's daughter, Sarah Grascome. What became of the feltmaking shop is not known. It is unlikely that it was pulled down, for Butler seems to have had plans to extend or repair it. He had building materials listed on his inventory, '24 new Joysts, a wyartree and other wood . . . brick and tiles'.[12] Was the workshop intended for the nineteen-year-old Thomas Bracebridge?

As Samuel Bracebridge had seemingly contrived the marriage of his daughter, Susanna, to the son of feltmaker, Samuel Butler, he might have

---

[10] Bracebridge papers: Abraham Bracebridge and Martha Blore *v.* Shem Bracebridge *et al.*, 1694, CR258/432, W.C.R.O.

[11] Will of Abraham Bracebridge, 1692, CR258/229, W.C.R.O.

[12] Probate inventory, L.J.R.O. B/C/11, Samuel Butler, 1664.

hoped eventually to acquire control of Butler's feltmaking concern. Whether he did or not we may never know. Certainly the Bracebridges did acquire property in Hartshill during the late seventeenth century, but its exact location remains uncertain. With a ready supply of spring water, Mill Lane Close would have been ideally situated for a feltmaking business, and indeed, in the following century it appears that a nearby property was taken over by John Wilday, the Bracebridges' successor, and adapted for the mechanical carding of wool.[13] Abraham's will itemises a 'Messuage cottage or tenement Closes Lands Rents Tyths and hereditaments . . . with their Appurtenances . . . in Hartshill', all of which were left to Thomas.[14] But Thomas, still an apprentice, was not destined to take on his father's entrepreneurial interests as a haberdasher of hats, because he died on 14th August 1695, just a few months after his father. This left the third son, Abraham, as heir. He had inherited land at Austrey, but to run the business he needed Atherstone Hall and its warehouses, which had been left to Samuel, the eldest son, who was now set on a parliamentary career, and had no interest in making hats.

In 1696 Samuel sold Atherstone Hall to Abraham for £400.[15] Their mother, Mary, was still living there, and stayed on for a while to help and support her youngest son. Later she went to live with her daughter, Susanna Atkins, at Horninghold in Leicestershire, where she died in 1701. She had obviously found it a strain, at the centre of a family row, for in her will she expressed a desire 'to leave things in quietness' and to be buried in the grave of her late, 'dear', husband, at Mancetter.[16]

Samuel Bracebridge married Anne Savage of Malvern in Worcestershire in 1697 and set about 'improving' Lindley manor. He imported an army of builders to remodel the house in the classical style. Had Samuel shown restraint and left the house alone it might well have survived to this day. An ancient fortified manor house complete with moat, and originally set in a woodland clearing, it was more typical of the Warwickshire Arden than of Leicestershire. Samuel decided that the gothic turrets were old-fashioned and inappropriate for the residence of a gentleman.[17] This was

---

[13] Order Book of the New Fire Office of London, 25 March, 1797, CR1039/1, W.C.R.O.

[14] Will of Abraham Bracebridge, 1692, CR258/229, W.C.R.O.

[15] Bracebridge papers: Conveyance by lease and release, Atherstone Hall and Lands, Samuel Bracebridge to Abraham Bracebridge, 9–10 September, 1696, CR258/5, W.C.R.O.

[16] Will of Mary Bracebridge, 1701, CR258/232, W.C.R.O.

[17] J. Nichols, *The History and Antiquities of the County of Leicester, Vol. IV, Part II* (London, 1795, reprinted 1971), facing p. 641.

not an unusual view. It has been said that there was 'no market in second-hand mansions in eighteenth-century England'.[18] Following the fashion of the age, Samuel pulled down the old house and rebuilt it with Palladio firmly in his mind. He embellished the new classical facade with a two-storey portico, topped by a triangular pediment and supported on four Ionic columns. The garden front received similar treatment with a domed half-circular pavilion, supported on four columns, to provide a second grand entrance.[19] The park was laid out in the natural landscape style which would later become associated with Capability Brown, and stocked with deer and hare to provide sport for gentlemen. This would have been impractical at Atherstone, where the cottages of the town jostled the palings of the park, encouraging poachers.

Whilst his elder brother was directing workmen and consulting the fashionable texts of Palladio, Abraham was learning the rudiments of trade at Atherstone Hall. It was fortunate that, along with the hatmaking business, he had inherited his father's two loyal servants, John Martin and Abraham Muston, who with his mother, were able to guide him through his early days. But, before long, Abraham was well able to stand on his own two feet. He quickly learned everything that his elders could teach him. The Bracebridges' flair for business was in his blood. He was further helped by the prevailing economic climate, in which Britain, under Queen Anne, was enjoying a period of peace and prosperity, with expanding trade both at home and abroad. Soon he was in a position to marry and chose Cecily Byrd of Claybrook in Leicestershire.

Socially this was not a brilliant marriage, for the Byrds, by their actions, had made themselves very unpopular with the county gentry. Cecily's father, William, had bought the mansion house at Claybrook in 1670. In 1681, with the sort of insensitivity we have come to associate more with the Bracebridges, he had claimed wasteland and commons at Little Claybrook as his own, and given the local people good reason to name the gales which occurred in 1703 as 'Byrd's wind'.[20] Byrd was bitterly aware of their dislike of him. In his will, written in April of that year, he added a precautionary clause, 'I Desire to be Buried in ye Night or Evening with all privacy'.[21]

It was said that William was 'the first of the family of any note who,

---

[18] H. J. Habakkuk, 'England', in *The European Nobility in the Eighteenth Century*, ed. A. Goodwin (London, 1953), p. 3.

[19] Nichols, *Vol. IV, Part II*, facing p. 647.

[20] Nichols, *Vol. IV, Part I*, p. 104.

[21] Will of William Byrd, 1703, CR258/259, W.C.R.O.

from a mean pedigree and estate was brought up to law as a barrister', but showed 'little reading and no modesty.' To make matters worse his brother, Thomas, had contrived the arrest of a popular royalist sympathiser, William Paul, a Church of England clergyman, who supported the Pretender. Paul was executed for high treason, and for the betrayal of his so-called 'friend', Byrd became known as 'Kill Parson'. From then on the Byrd family never prospered, and indeed Cecily's marriage to Abraham in 1699 gave a foretaste of this, for it was short and ill-fated, and Abraham himself was never to achieve the success he so desperately sought.[22]

The Byrds knew Atherstone well, for William also owned the neighbouring manor of Witherley, which would come to Abraham after his death. Busy with the activity of weavers and framework knitters, Cecily's home village of Claybrook prepared her well for life in a small industrial centre. Close to Watling Street, it was one of the open villages where industrial occupation flourished. Indeed William Byrd was probably engaged in some trading activity himself, for in his will, he leaves five pounds to his apprentice, 'When he is out of his Time provided that in the Interim he behave himself as he ought.'

Cecily and Abraham enjoyed very little happiness together. Within a year of marriage they had buried their first child, Mary. Two years later a son was born. By naming him William, after his maternal grandfather, they had unwittingly sealed his fate, for his life, too, was brief. One can imagine how the death of Cecily's first child would have overshadowed the upbringing of her second. Constantly fearful for his safety, she would have kept a watchful eye on him as he played. It was impossible to keep a toddler away from the yard with the incessant to and fro of the putting out system. Cecily watched carts arriving frequently, clattering on the cobbles, laden with wool and dyes from foreign parts, followed by an equally noisy dispatch of crates filled with hats. When, accompanied by her maid, she ventured into the town, the smell of steamy wool and sweat would briefly assault her nostrils as she passed the cottages in the market place. A glimpse of glistening torsos labouring over the feltmaker's kettle met her eye when doors were open, but she was unlikely to have been offended by such honest labour. Indeed, it was difficult to maintain a delicacy about the realities of human life when they were in such close proximity. Abraham, for his part, was proud of his enterprise. Like many eighteenth-century entrepreneurs who built their factories in full view of their mansions, relishing the sight of smoking chimneys, he was happy to

---

[22] Nichols, *Vol. IV, Part I*, p. 104.

share his home with his business. Industry had not yet defaced the countryside, and no-one at that date could have envisaged how, within a hundred years, it would change the landscape irrevocably. At that time there was nothing incongruous about an elegant country mansion housing a trade. Before the advent of factory-based industry all commercial enterprise took place in a domestic setting. It was no more unusual to have a warehouse holding hats within the curtilage of one's home than it was a barn storing grain or hay. It was an accepted part of life that industry and husbandry co-existed in cottage and mansion. There was no stigma attached to trade, and the distaste which the middle classes would later feel for the means of creating their wealth had not yet developed.

Atherstone Hall stood a little to the north of the market place, convenient for the feltmakers who lived in the small cottages which lined the square. Within the Hall was a warehouse where Abraham kept a stock of wool, dyestuffs and trimming materials. Here the wool was weighed out in small quantities and delivered to, or collected by, the cottage feltmakers. This piecework system of putting out materials to outside labour was forbidden in London, where feltmaking was carried out in a master's shop by employed journeymen. In the country, the feltmaker would take away enough wool for a week's work of about a dozen hats. The number he was able to produce depended upon the season of the year and the demands of the land. When he had worked his wool into felt hoods in the workshop attached to his house, perhaps sharing resources with other feltmakers, he would return them to Atherstone Hall, where Bracebridge would pay him for his labour.

The scale of the Bracebridge operation is evident from the probate inventory attached to his father's will, written in 1694.[23] He left 'Wool, Galls, Logwood, &c.' to the value of £317 4s. 8d., 'Hatts in the Hatt chamber' amounted to £380 19s. 10d. 'Hatt linings and bands &c.' came to £312 3s. 10d. Debts owed to Bracebridge amounted to well over £4000. This by any standard was an enormous business, perhaps the largest of all the English provincial hatting operations.

Of course, Abraham Bracebridge was not a 'master', for he did not stand in the relationship of a skilled craftsman towards his journeymen and apprentices. He was a merchant, and although Atherstone Hall housed the facility for weighing out wool, with the possibility of dyeing, stiffening and finishing, and the certainty of warehousing, the feltmaking itself was all done in small cottage workshops, by men who were probably of equal

---

[23] Inventory of Abraham Bracebridge, 1694, CR258/261, W.C.R.O.

Item Hatts in the Hatt chamber — CCCiiijxx: xijli: ad

Item Hatt linings and bands &c — xxxij:iij:x:

Item Goods in the Warehouse — iiij:

Item Debts sperate in the shop books — MCCCxxvi xiiij: iiijd

Item Debts sperate for Rent in arrear — CCCCxxvij: xli vijd

Item Debts sperate on spetialty — MDCClxxij: vijli iijd

Item Desperate Debts on spetialty — CCCiiijxxxxiiij xvjli vijd

Summa totalis hujus Inventarij — MDCCiiijxx: jli jxd

8. Detail of Inventory of Abraham Bracebridge, 1692.

status, and may not have served formal apprenticeships. No dyers or dyeshops are mentioned in the late seventeenth century probate inventories for Mancetter, and it would seem that either Abraham's own 'servants' dyed the hats on his premises, or the dye was put out with the hat to local dyers who have left no records. The dyestuffs shown on Abraham's inventory, 'Galls, Logwood &c.', would have produced only the browns and blacks suitable for coarse country felts, and would not have been over-demanding on the skills of the dyer. It is not until the early eighteenth century that we find records of hatters who were also dyeing.

Richard Payne was an independent hatter who died in 1711. His probate inventory shows how the cottage trade was developing alongside Brace-bridge's, with premises gradually expanding to cover all stages of manu-facture.[24] Payne rented a house which had an integral shop where finished hats were stored and probably retailed. Adjoining was a 'Working Shop', equipped with a 'Coulouring Kettle, 5 Basons, Blocks, Hurdle and Bowes', where the bowing, basoning and dyeing was done. Next to this was a 'Walk Shop', equipped with 'The Kettle, planks & 2 old Forms'. The furnace beneath the kettle was not mentioned as it would have been one of the fixtures of the building. Payne owned wool to the value of £2, indicating that he was making hats on his own account rather than for Bracebridge.

Payne's hats would have been trimmed by his wife, Dorothy, in the same way that the trimming of Bracebridge's hats was probably put out to the wives of his feltmakers. Until recent years it was common to see women carrying away from the factories large black bags, bulky with hats and trimmings. The women would have visited Atherstone Hall, to collect hat linings and bands, with which to trim the hats at home. The completed hats were packed into crates and taken away by cart, some to local towns, and inevitably some to London, where they would soon find a market amongst the ranks of Queen Anne's armed forces.

There was another facet of the Bracebridge enterprise. Before the arrival of joint-stock banks it was left to wealthy individuals with business interests to provide finance for other people's enterprises. Much of the wealth that Abraham Bracebridge I amassed from his hatting business was loaned out on bond, by deed, or 'specialty'. An agreement was drawn up between the two parties and an interest rate was fixed. It was then signed, sealed and witnessed, and the bond held by the lender. Repayments would usually be due on the quarter days of the year, Lady Day, Midsummer,

---

[24] Probate inventory, L.J.R.O. B/C/11, Richard Payne, 1711.

Michaelmas and Epiphany. When all payments had been made the bond was returned to the borrower or destroyed.

When Abraham Bracebridge I died in 1694 he left £1767 in 'debts sperate on specialty' – these were the secure debts which he had hope of having repaid. Then there was an amount of £393 in 'Desperate Debts on specialty' – unsecured debts for which he had little hope of receiving repayment. Abraham, it appears, was acting in the role of a banker, perhaps to local people, who needed money for various purposes, and because their security was poor, would have to pay high interest rates. He could also have been financing the sale of his own goods by loaning money to the retailers and merchants who would distribute the hats. At his death, apart from the 'sperate' and 'desperate' debts, he was also owed £1481 in 'Debts sperate on the shop books'. These would be the day-to-day trading debts owed by his customers, as opposed to those for which bonds were drawn up. Then there were the 'Debts sperate for Rent in arrear', which was the income from property he owned. The ever-present threat of eviction hung over these people, so they would not be tardy in paying their debts.

Although, by the time of his death, Abraham Bracebridge I's business had grown considerably, during the proto-industrial age, it was not practical for it to grow beyond a manageable size. Thus, when capital built up there arose the question of what should be done with it. Whilst Abraham Bracebridge I seems to have confined his financial dealings to those of a specialised banker, his son would solve the problem by investing in land.

Wealth made in trade would enable a man to add dealing in money and in credit to his other business activities.[25] It would probably be necessary to add a counter to his office, to handle financial transactions, and it might often happen that finance overtook trade as the major business. But although they were undoubtedly acting as bankers, it was not the Bracebridge family which set up Atherstone's first country bank, but the Wildays, who were to accumulate large profits from the hat industry when they took it over later in the eighteenth century.

Obviously, the Bracebridges had long had trading links with London through the purchase of imported wool and dyestuffs, and the sale of hats. Soon they would begin to diversify their investments there, into sugar-refining, bullion, insurance and banking, and would purchase a substantial London residence in Lincoln's Inn Fields.

---

[25] P. Mathias, *The First Industrial Nation: The Economic History of Britain 1700–1914*, 2nd edition (London, 1983), pp. 151–3.

CHAPTER 6

Abraham Bracebridge II:
The Fight For Enclosure

CECILY'S UNTIMELY DEATH in 1707 left Abraham Bracebridge II with a heavy heart and a son aged five. He became reclusive, aloof from his fellow townsmen and unyielding in his dealings with them. He had few interests outside business which continued to prosper under his astute management. It was necessary to marry again, as soon as practicable, for his son needed a mother. It was also prudent to produce more heirs as an insurance against the epidemics which swept the town from time to time, taking with them the lives of the least resistant, the very young and the very old.

It took Abraham four years to find a second wife. Mary Jennings, twenty-seven and five years his junior, was the daughter of a clergyman from Little Onne in Staffordshire. This was a very different match from his first marriage in which Cecily's father had settled for a jointure of only one hundred pounds a year. Mary's family was not so obliging. They tied Abraham down to a tight marriage settlement, in which he had to convey all his property into a trust to provide for his wife and any future children. He signed this on 12th April 1710, and was married soon after. The marriage articles itemise Abraham's property holdings at that date.[1] He would go down in the local records as the man whose greed for land led him into unscrupulous and reprehensible behaviour towards his fellow townsmen. In 1710 that greed was not yet evident.

Apart from a 'new erected Messuage' (possibly the dower house to Atherstone Hall, known today as Chapel House), the marriage articles show Abraham as holding eight and a half yardlands. At an estimate of twenty-five acres per yardland, this amounted to approximately 212 acres.[2] Under the open field system these yardlands were divided into strips,

---

[1] Indenture between Abraham Bracebridge, Walter Jennings, Mary Jennings, Walter Yonge and George Greenway, on marriage, 12 April 1710, CR258/203, W.C.R.O.

[2] The acreage of a yardland was not fixed, but tended to be an area upon which a household could subsist. Thus it varied from manor to manor, according to soil quality.

'promiscuously dispersed in the several fields of Atherston'. All this land, plus a few odd acres, was leased out to local people. Abraham had the reputation of being 'a tradesman and no great farmer', in fact, he farmed no land himself.[3] The marriage articles also include copyhold property, namely a house, 'situated upon the hill in the Long Street in Atherstone' (today No. 180 Long Street), and a yardland in the open fields. To transfer it into the trust, under the custom of the manor, Abraham attended the customary court and first surrendered the property into the hands of the lord of the manor. After payment of a fine, the lord of the manor, or as was more usual, his steward, passed the property to the trust.

Abraham and Mary began their marriage 'living over the shop' in Atherstone Hall. Their first child, Mary, was baptised at Mancetter Church on 5 April 1711. She was to be small consolation for the loss of William two weeks later, aged eight. He may have died of smallpox, which was a frequent visitor to Atherstone. It was two years before another son, Walter, was born, and like William, named after his maternal grandfather. A second son followed in 1716, and by christening him Abraham his father unwittingly identified him as his heir.

The early years of the eighteenth century were good times for the hatters. Queen Anne's campaign in Belgium ensured that hats were required for the soldiers who fought under Marlborough at the Battle of Blenheim. This period also saw the rise of the slave trade. Packed into the holds of Africa-bound slaving ships, cheap Atherstone felts shared space with trinkets from Birmingham and other goods sold in Africa to buy slaves. The unfortunate captives were each equipped with a hat to shield their heads from the elements during the nightmare voyage, and at their destination to protect them from the fierce sun as they slaved on the white man's sugar plantations. So prosperous was this trade that the Bracebridge family were to acquire a substantial interest in the 'Sugar houses'.[4]

But, however well regarded was the eighteenth-century tradesman entrepreneur, he could not achieve social status without the possession of an estate. Land conferred the right to vote and to stand for election to the House of Commons. Abraham's father had been Sheriff of Warwickshire in 1694, but this was an administrative office. The true county power resided with the justices of the peace. In 1716 it became apparent that Abraham Bracebridge was set upon the acquisition of land. In that year he commissioned a map and a survey of landholding in

---

[3] The case of Atherstone concerning Inclosure of Common Fields, January 1738, HR35/25, W.C.R.O.

[4] Will of Abraham Bracebridge, 8 September 1789, CR258/259, W.C.R.O.

Atherstone.[5] This provided him with an itemised catalogue of land which he could attempt to acquire for himself, as and when the opportunity arose.

He was thirty-eight with a growing family, and no doubt becoming tired of the day-to-day business of hatmaking, which although profitable, did little to enhance his standing in county society. His new marriage and young family should have brought him happiness, but instead he had become ill-tempered, withdrawn and misanthropic. He spent long hours in his study, poring over property deeds and wills, and learning more than any man before him had ever known about landholding in the manor of Atherstone. He was meticulous in record keeping, always retaining copies of his correspondence, which shows him to be a 'forceful, domineering and generally unattractive personality'.[6] If this was not enough, the same writer also described him as 'a devious and mean plotter . . . easily irritated by delay'. A field map, commissioned by Bracebridge in 1716, shows that in the six years since his marriage his holding of land in the three open fields had risen from 212 acres to 303, almost half of the total area under plough. What is particularly surprising is that, as a mere freeholder and copyholder, Bracebridge was able to acquire so much land. Obviously the lord of the manor did not have any aspirations to extend his manor from the five yardlands (roughly 125 acres) which it comprised in 1661. Indeed, his holding would shrink dramatically, for by 1765 the manor was to own only seven acres, the balance having fallen into Bracebridge hands. With an apathetic lord of the manor it was not difficult for a strong and determined personality to force his will on local people, especially as he had taken their part in previous disputes with manor officials, and had thereby won their confidence.

One of Bracebridge's first moves was to get hold of the manorial records, the 'Town books and writings'.[7] He never attempted any action without thorough preparation, and possession of all the available information on landholding in the manor was a prerequisite of his plan to enfranchise his copyhold land so that it became freehold. Copyhold land carried with it an obligation to pay annual dues to the lord of the manor, and it is likely that Bracebridge came to some agreement with Edward Repington to enfranchise the copyhold by purchase, and free the land

---

[5] A Plan of Atherstone Feildes, Robert Hewitt, 1716, P7, W.C.R.O.

[6] M. J. Kingman, 'Landlord v. Community: The Bracebridge Family and the Enclosure of Atherstone Open Fields, 1730–1765', in *Warwickshire History, Vol. VII, No. 4* (Winter 1988/9), p. 90.

[7] Watts & Winyard, p. 33.

from this liability. Probably the lord of the manor welcomed the prop-
osition as a way of raising cash, which could be invested to yield a better
return than the lesser amount he received annually.

During the following years Bracebridge's greed for land and power
became obsessive. Within the rich archive which he has left to us, and
which lies today in the vaults of the Warwickshire County Record Office,
are many documents concerning the land and property of Atherstone
people. There are copies of their wills, bequeathing to their families various
parcels of land, which Bracebridge was anxious to appropriate for himself.
Subsequently some of these holdings are found in Bracebridge's possession.
One will in particular was that of Francis Gramer of Kenilworth in
Warwickshire, who died in 1730, leaving extensive property in two
counties to his 'Loveing wife, Frances'.[8] Hardly allowing for a decent
period to elapse, Bracebridge approached the grieving widow and secured
a large slice of her property which included a farm house with adjoining
buildings two yard lands and other copyhold land, for £170.[9] Part of the
land carried with it an obligation to pay £5 a year to the poor, and
Bracebridge managed to indemnify himself against this charge, leaving it
as Mrs Gramer's responsibility.[10]

Amongst Bracebridge's papers are lists of property holdings in Atherstone, spanning the years between 1661 and 1730.[11] These were drawn
from the manor records, still in his possession. By 1730 Bracebridge owned
three-quarters of Atherstone's land and was eligible to apply for an act of
parliament to enclose the open fields.

Until the prospect of enclosure loomed over the townsfolk, eighteenth-
century Atherstone had enjoyed prosperity, drawing people from far and
wide to share in the good standard of living which was the consequence
of generous rights of common and growing opportunities for trade. Houses
were fully occupied and any vacancy was quickly filled. There were
twenty-three freeholders holding land in the open fields and living by a
combination of trade and husbandry. The cottagers, 'or tradesmen of a
lower rank', although landless, also enjoyed a reasonable standard of living.
One source of income was feltmaking, but it was necessary to find other

---

[8] Will of Francis Gramer, 1730, CR258/259, W.C.R.O.
[9] Agreement between Frances Gramer and Abraham Bracebridge, 1731, MR/9/62,
W.C.R.O.
[10] Kingman, p. 90.
[11] Rent Rolls for the Manor of Atherstone, 1661 and undated, MR9/11 and MR9/14,
W.C.R.O.

work to tide them over 'in a dull time of Trade'.[12] Grazing rights enabled cottagers to keep a horse and cart to fetch coals or ply for hire. The poorest could find work as farm labourers, tilling the soil of the better off.

The majority were sympathetic towards the landless cottagers. When enclosure was first mooted they opposed it for the effect it would have on those who depended upon common rights for their livelihood. But Bracebridge was determined to get his own way. In February 1730 he prepared a list of possible arbitrators, who would be appointed to consider the merits of the case and see enclosure implemented, for if there was sufficient support, an act of parliament would not be necessary. These 'neighbouring gentlemen' were said to be 'wholly disinterested in the affair, and above being influenced by any person or party'.[13] The seven named were all on visiting terms with Bracebridge. One was a relative by marriage, and another the father-in-law of Mancetter's lay impropriator of tithes. The support of any falterers, who included the lord of the manor, was secured by persuasion and bribery. However, despite his efforts, Bracebridge did not achieve enclosure by agreement and the matter was dropped for five years.

In 1735 he tried again, but this time through an act of parliament. There was a new list of sponsors, including the lord of the manor and his son, and the four largest landholders, including Bracebridge. Another is an upwardly mobile member of a feltmaking family, John Ragdale, a clerk in holy orders, living in Nottingham, whose father and grandfather had both been cottage feltmakers, possibly working for Bracebridge. At one time they had a substantial holding in the open fields, but when John moved away from Atherstone he began to sell land to Bracebridge. His younger brother, Samuel, remained in Atherstone and continued as a feltmaker. His name appears on a list 'for a Jury' to look into the merits of enclosure in 1738.[14] Also on this list is Joseph Wilday, who within four years would be described as a 'haberdasher of hats', and was already beginning to collect property for himself. Finally, the 'jury' included the impropriator of tithes, who would benefit from increased rents after

---

[12] Paper of Grievances, c. 1736, HR35/10, W.C.R.O.

[13] Copy of letter naming commissioners, 9 February 1730, HR35/1, W.C.R.O. These were: 'Esq. Chetwynd of Grendon, Esq. Wright of Caldecott, Esq. Stratford of Merevale, Mr Dugdale of Blythe, Mr Ludford of Ancely, Mr Muxloe of Swepstone, Mr Hodges of Caldecoat'. John Bracebridge Ludford (1707–75) was a cousin, and Muxlow's daughter, Mary (1712–76), was married to Thomas Clare, lay impropriator of tithes in the parish of Mancetter.

[14] Names for a Jury, 26 August 1738, HR35/19, W.C.R.O.

enclosure, raising the suspicion that Bracebridge used his influence to rig this jury.

One would imagine that those who faced the most acute dilemma were the cottagers who depended upon Bracebridge for work in hatmaking. Each cottage was asked to pay £1 towards the fighting fund, which was a considerable slice of the family's average income of £22 a year, and would have marked them out openly as opponents.[15] However, it may be that the variety of means by which cottagers could earn their living, and the independence which common rights conferred, encouraged them to stand up to Bracebridge. After all, in a year of good harvest, he needed their labour (which no doubt was bought at a cheap price) more than they needed his money. During the 1730s, until 1739, harvest yields had been good, and it was said that 'the labouring people lived well'.[16] Meat was cheap and no doubt industrious people on manors with generous rights of common would have been well off.

Bracebridge was forced to use intimidatory measures to try and dissuade the cottagers from opposing him. He cancelled the annual horse races, held on the 'Race Meadow' in the open fields, and had them moved to Nuneaton, 'in order to distress the Town and force them into Compliance'.[17] He also collected together some of the neighbouring gentry, and mounted on horses, they set out to 'startle some of the opponents'.[18] It is easy to imagine the sort of language that was used to frighten them. In fact, in an age when the average man had no voice in politics, Bracebridge would have been most annoyed and frustrated to find that the poorest members of the community could have some say in the matter of enclosure, and might even have the temerity to defy him. There is a suggestion that Bracebridge was threatened, and 'obliged to keep a guard on himself and his family'.[19] This was a rare situation in a country manor and even more remarkable if account is also taken of Bracebridge's role in providing local employment.

The verdict of the jury, which met in late summer 1738, is not recorded, but it appears to have been inclined towards enclosure, for a bill was drafted in early October. Then, on November 6th, in a last ditch attempt to stop the bill's progress, seventy-seven of Atherstone's inhabitants

---

[15] Cottagers answer to paper entitled 'Inclosure Vindicated', c.1738, HR35/15, W.C.R.O.

[16] Dorothy Marshall, *Eighteenth-Century England* (London, 1962, reprint 1985), p. 474.

[17] The Case of Atherstone concerning Inclosure of the Common Fields, January 1738, HR35/25, W.C.R.O.

[18] Letter from Tho. Lovell, Lichfield, 8 October 1738, HR35/22, W.C.R.O.

[19] E. P. Thompson, *Customs in Common* (London, 1991), p. 154.

appointed two London attorneys to oppose it.[20] Their success marked the end of the enclosure debate which was not reopened for almost thirty years.

Despite his wealth, and the unscrupulous use of power, Abraham Bracebridge had not achieved his dearest ambition. But, unable to concede defeat, he continued to buy up land when the opportunity arose. In 1740 he paid John Ragdale £385 for a house and burgage with outbuildings, and a yardland in the open fields. The sitting tenant remained, paying rent of seven pence to Bracebridge. The price paid for the yardland was amongst the highest ever, and transactions of this order were soon to take their toll on Abraham Bracebridge II.[21] The long and expensive campaign to try and procure an act of enclosure, together with an insatiable greed for land, had decimated his fortune. This obsession had also diverted his attention from his business, which was still largely managed by his servant, the feltmaker, Joseph Hatton, helped by Abraham's elder son, Walter, who was then in his mid twenties.

Abraham's last will, written about the time he bought John Ragdale's property, is a sad contrast to the will of his father. He had settled portions of £1000 on each of his three younger children.[22] But the money was running out fast, and when he died in 1744, the estate was insufficient to pay either the legacies or the debts.

It was left to Abraham's eldest son, Walter, to pay off these debts. He was a young man with a strong sense of responsibility and a gentle nature, unusual in a Bracebridge man. In 1741 Walter had married Theodosia Church of Tunstall in Staffordshire. As was usual, the marriage settlement gave the family an opportunity to rearrange its property. Atherstone Hall, Witherley manor (which had come to the family from William Byrd through his daughter's marriage) and other properties and lands were settled on Walter and Theodosia. Her jointure was divided between Walter and his father, Abraham. Like his grandfather, Abraham Bracebridge I, on his marriage Walter was made a co-partner of the business. Within forty days of his wedding he had to agree to pay his father half the value of the 'goods, wares and merchandise, utensils and implements . . . belonging to the trade or . . . mistery of a wholesale habberdasher of Hatts'.[23] His

---

[20] Kingman, p. 93.

[21] Indenture between John Ragdale and Abraham Bracebridge, 1740, MR9/6, W.C.R.O.

[22] Will of Abraham Bracebridge, 6 March 1740, CR258/259, W.C.R.O.

[23] Marriage settlement by lease and release between Walter Bracebridge and Theodosia Church, 18–19 January 1741, CR258/209–210, W.C.R.O.

cousin, Samuel, of Lindley Hall was one of the settlement trustees, holding the settled property to the use of Walter and Theodosia.

It was a marriage of love, and when she died just eleven months later, he was devastated. As a tribute to Theodosia's 'exemplary humility and sweetness of temper' he commissioned a memorial to her in Mancetter church. It speaks eloquently of his devotion and his grief. 'She lived beloved, and died lamented, but especially by her disconsolate husband, who, as the least token of his unspeakable grief caused to be erected this monument of his never dying love.'

His hopes and happiness destroyed, Walter drew up his own will. The tone is bitter and full of resentment for his father's inexcusable profligacy.[24] It seems that his only remaining wish was to satisfy his father's creditors and ensure that his two unmarried sisters, Mary and Elizabeth, received their inheritance. But the problems which Walter was left to sort out were longstanding. Abraham's debts stretched back to his mother's death, when he had failed to pay his daughter, Mary, a legacy of £850, left by her grandmother, and had used the money for his own purposes. Walter had to find this sum, plus the £1000 portions promised by his father, and, if that was not enough, he had to pay off his father's debts. Having done all that he had no wish to return to Atherstone Hall to take over as his father's heir. Within two weeks of Abraham's death Walter had leased the mansion and its adjacent property to Francis Stratford of Merevale.[25]

Walter survived his young wife by only five years, dying on January 3rd 1747, aged thirty-three, a dispirited man. His estate was just sufficient to clear his father's debts, and leave a small residue for his brother, Abraham Bracebridge III, his father's true heir. Abraham would return to Atherstone Hall to continue the fight for enclosure and make the transition to true gentrification by selling off the family's interest in trade.

---

[24] Will of Walter Bracebridge, 7 September 1743, CR258/259, W.C.R O.
[25] Lease by Walter Bracebridge of mansion house and inn, to Francis Stratford, 4 November 1743, CR258/25.

CHAPTER 7

A Changing Social Order:
The Rise of the Wildays

WHILST Abraham Bracebridge II was neglecting his putting-out business to pursue enclosure, a new generation of entrepreneur was awaiting the opportunity to usurp his position. In the seventeenth century the Wildays had been landless cottagers, but within a hundred years they had climbed a few rungs of the social ladder and achieved a position of some influence in the local community.

Upward mobility in that period, as today, was conditional upon economic success. By the craft of their hands or a prudent marriage it was just possible for a family of landless cottagers to rise, in a couple of generations, to a position of wealth and social standing. The first step might be to apprentice a son, perhaps with the help of a wealthy sponsor, to a master craftsman in a City livery company. His apprenticeship finished, and established as a journeyman, the son might attract the daughter of a merchant, who would bring a good dowry to the marriage. This would enable him to set up as a master in his own right. The profits of his trade would be invested in property. Then, by and by, he might purchase a small estate, which would give him social standing, and allow him to enter the ranks of the 'middling sort'. This was the route taken by the Wildays, who in the 1650s had been cottage feltmakers working for Bracebridge. Thomas Wilday, who died in 1690, left possessions valued at a total of £38 10s. 6d. His rented house contained three rooms and a feltmaker's workshop.[1]

Although Thomas was a man of modest means, he had been singled out from his peers when he was appointed sheriff's bailiff. He had also sent his son, Samuel, aged seventeen, to London to be apprenticed to a member of the Worshipful Company of Feltmakers.[2] Samuel served eight years before qualifying as a journeyman hatter. Perhaps Abraham

---

[1] See Chapter Four.
[2] Feltmakers' Court Minute Book, May 1682, GL Ms 1570/1.

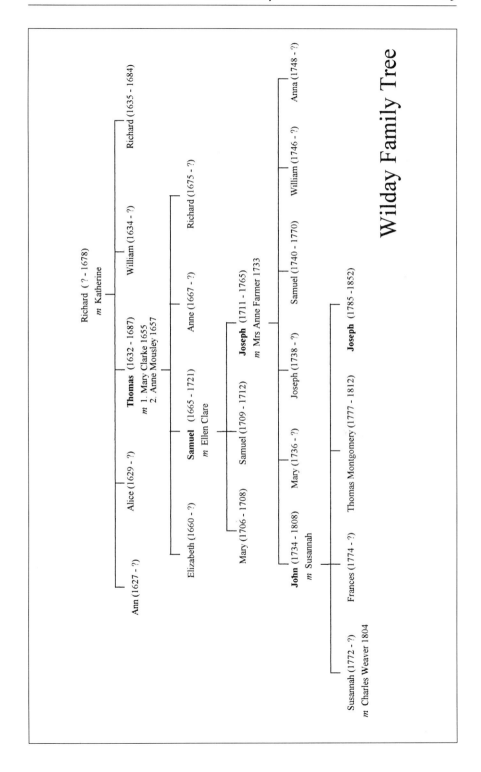

Wilday Family Tree

Bracebridge I sponsored him, for the costs of apprenticing a boy to a London master were usually beyond the means of ordinary folk, and it was more usual for the sons of well-established tradesmen or the lesser gentry to receive such training.

Samuel evidently prospered and was able to make a good marriage. Ellen Clare's family were shoemakers, who were themselves upwardly mobile. Her cousin, Thomas Clare, was influential enough to become the lay impropriator of tithes for the parish of Mancetter. Although Samuel and Ellen produced three children, only Joseph, born in 1711, survived to adulthood.[3]

By this time Samuel was Atherstone's most important feltmaker. He attracted the sons of the well-to-do as his apprentices. Amongst them was William Reeve the son of a dyer and citizen of London, whose family paid £9 10s. 0d. in 1715 to bind him to Samuel for the customary seven years.[4] Unhappily, Samuel died before the boy completed his apprenticeship. As was usual when a son was under age, Samuel's widow, Ellen, carried on the feltmaking trade until Joseph was old enough to take responsibility himself. A few days after his death, an inventory of Samuel's goods was drawn up by his friends. It itemises, 'Stock in hatts and wooll Copperas & Logwood £46 0s. 0d., more hatts in ye Press, Tools in the Shop, Bow Strings at £10 0s. 0d.'. The presence of logwood and copperas (sulphate of copper was used with logwood to make a black dye) indicates that Wilday also dyed his hats. His house, which he owned, comprised four rooms, 'A Dwelling house, Parlour, chamber of ye house and chamber of ye Parlour', plus 'Backside, gardens and . . . premises'. His trading debts both 'Sperate and Desperate' come to £201 0s. 0d., and include, 'Muck in ye yard'. In total Samuel Wilday left goods valued at £396 7s. 10d.[5]

Samuel's will makes clear that he was depending upon Ellen to continue the business. But, if not, he asks, 'That she will sell and Dispose of all the utensills and working Tooles belonging to (his) shop and Trade to the best advantage she can.' Joseph was only ten at the time, and too young to be considering a career. However, after Ellen's death all Samuel's property, including money due on mortgages, was to come to Joseph. In addition, at his coming of age, he was to receive the sum of £50.[6]

---

[3] Mancetter Parish Register records the births as follows: Mary, 26 December 1706, Samuel, 25 February 1708/9, Joseph, 6 December 1711, DR130/1, W.C.R.O.

[4] I am grateful to Mr F. B. Withers for this reference.

[5] Probate inventory, L.J.R.O. B/C/11, Samuel Wilday, 1721.

[6] Will, L.J.R.O. B/C/11, Samuel Wilday, 1721.

It does not take much imagination to put oneself into the position of Ellen Wilday, left comfortably off by her husband, but inordinately fond of her one surviving child. When Joseph was old enough she sent him to London to take an apprenticeship with a haberdasher of hats, so that he could become a merchant and enter the trade at the highest level. Before he went to London, he would have learned the rudiments of feltmaking by watching his mother's journeymen. One can picture him, a small boy, standing beside the feltmaker as he bowed the wool, perhaps being allowed to try for himself, or standing on tiptoes to look into the kettle as the men worked at the plank. In London he would have learned how to buy wool, to assess its quality, and how to fix a tight rate with the feltmakers. As a wholesaler he would need to develop links with retailers and understand the economics of the commercial world.

Joseph came home in the early 1730s full of ideas and eager to prove himself. Nationally it was a time of peace and good harvests, but in Atherstone things were not so good. People were experiencing the greatest crisis the town had ever known. The fear that the open fields would be enclosed united them in the fight to prevent Bracebridge from obtaining an act of parliament. No-one could settle to work on the land or at their trade. The fight diverted many of the townsfolk's energies and blighted the town, discouraging prosperous settlers, who had been drawn to Atherstone by the generous common rights attached to properties. When Bracebridge failed, the enclosure issue was dropped for thirty years and life returned to normal, without the threat of the townsfolk losing the foundation of their livelihood. Prosperity returned, based upon the growth of trade and manufacturing, of which feltmaking was the major industry. The population increase in Atherstone was greater than anywhere else in Warwickshire at this time, as people were drawn to the town for the prospects it offered.[7]

George II had come to the throne in 1727 and had overcome his initial mistrust of Walpole, who was set upon protecting the interests of Britain's economy and, in particular, those of her manufacturers. He had removed import duties on raw materials which helped the feltmakers who, in general, purchased their wool from Spain, Portugal, Italy and the East. Furthermore, Walpole did not shirk from introducing protectionist measures when manufacturing interests were under threat. In 1732 he effectively banned the import of beaver hats from the American colonies. Instead they had to send beaver skins, so that the hats could be made in

---

[7] Watts and Winyard, p. 179.

Britain.[8] Thus the 1730s were a good time for the British hatting trade, and Joseph Wilday was ready to take advantage of the opportunities on offer.

In 1733, aged twenty-one, he finished his apprenticeship and married a comfortably-off widow, Ann Farmer. He took over the business which his mother had run in his absence and began work in Atherstone, in competition with Abraham Bracebridge. His training in London had taught him the commercial aspects of feltmaking. He was keen and innovative and soon became a match for Bracebridge, whose own interest in hat-making had been irretrievably diverted by his obsession with enclosure. Bracebridge's own putting out business had been delegated to his son, Walter, who had no heart for the trade, and his 'old servant' Joseph Hatton. Furthermore, Abraham Bracebridge II was financially a broken man, and may no longer have cared how his hatmaking business prospered. In addition to the money he had lost through imprudent land purchases, he may also have been suffering the effects of unfortunate investment in other areas of his commercial life. The economy was always subject to fluctuation from war and bad harvests, and since the speculative fever of the South Sea Bubble in 1718, the law on liability had been tightened so that any investor was personally responsible for the debts which a failed enterprise incurred.[9]

Meanwhile, Joseph Wilday was established as one of Atherstone's fore-most residents. In 1738, aged twenty-seven, he was asked to serve on the jury to decide on the outcome of the enclosure battle. He was beginning to build up his own property interests in Atherstone. Amongst his purchases was the copyhold on several houses on the south side of Long Street, well served by a watercourse, and so ideal for hatmaking. In fact, his grandson would build a model hat factory on the site. The family were also diversifying into other trades, including building and brickmaking.

Joseph and Ann produced eight children, but only three appear to have survived. The eldest, John, born in 1734, was to become a prosperous banker and hatmaker. His brother, Samuel, born in 1740, was also a man of enterprise and talent. By trade a builder, he also patented a revolutionary malt drying system. In April 1769 he entered into a contract with the Coventry Canal Company (in which he held six shares) to supervise the building of a section of the canal, under the engineer and surveyor, James Brindley.[10] That November, he sent Abraham Bracebridge III an estimate

[8] Marshall, p. 170.
[9] Mathias, p. 145.
[10] Watts and Winyard, pp. 78–80.

for a small building job. The obsequious tone shows that however prosperous the Wildays were becoming, they were not on equal terms with the Bracebridges:

> Saml Wildays most Respectful compliment to Mr Bracebridge as bricked up the Small cistern in Mr Freer's Yard as desired and will always do anything in his power to serve Mr Bracebridge has made an estimate of Enlarging the work which upon the most Moderate Computation will be £10 if agreeable to Mr Bracebridge . . .[11]

Samuel did not live to see the completion of his work on the canal. The following month he wrote his will, leaving everything to his youngest sister, Anna.[12] Within three years he was dead. In the local records, there is no mention of his elder brother, John, until the 1780s, suggesting that he was employed elsewhere, perhaps in a commercial house in London, where he was learning to become both a merchant and a banker. He may well have been taken under the wing of Abraham Bracebridge III, with a position in his London offices, where he was involved in a diversity of business interests ranging from insurance and hatting to sugar refining and soap making. Joseph Wilday's will, of February 1765, suggests that the relationship with his son, John, had broken off completely. Joseph left an estate at Berkswell, Warwickshire, to Samuel, and an estate in Witherley, Leicestershire, to his wife, Ann. She was also to inherit his Atherstone estate and his 'East India Stock'. John, who by then, is almost certainly involved with the Bracebridges, is not mentioned.[13] Could it be that Joseph had cut off his son for his connection with Bracebridge? The Bracebridges, too, would have resented Joseph's success, and having controlled the local hatmaking trade for four generations they would have done all in their power to extinguish the competition. Wilday, with his London training, was probably more dedicated and more efficient than the Bracebridges, whose interest in trade was flagging. What better reprisal than to steal Wilday's eldest son and to give him a share in their own business?

Local tradition says that Abraham Bracebridge III built a hat factory in the grounds of Atherstone Hall, and that John Wilday and another banker, John Chapman, were partners in the venture. Of course, for over a hundred years there had been a hat business based on Atherstone Hall. In 1692 it was contained in a 'Hat Chamber' and 'Warehouse', and in

---

[11] Letter from Samuel Wilday to Abraham Bracebridge, 4 November 1769, MR9/34, W.C.R.O.

[12] Copy of will of Samuel Wilday, 1770, CR2440/9/2, W.C.R.O.

[13] Copy of will of Joseph Wilday, 1765, CR2440/9/1, W.C.R.O.

1743, a 'Hat Chamber, Little Wooll Chamber, Packing Room and Work-house'.[14] This represents an expansion in line with the growth of the business. The addition of a 'Workhouse' suggests that some feltmaking or finishing was now carried out on the premises. Perhaps Abraham Brace-bridge II had begun feltmaking in house, following the gradual trend towards the factory system which would take place over the following fifty years. A natural progression would be the building of new premises to house further expansion. If Abraham was concentrating on the acquisi-tion of property, it is very likely that the youth he had groomed to manage the business had grown into a man he could trust as a partner.

After Abraham Bracebridge II died, the campaign for enclosure was carried on by his second son, Abraham III, who inherited the commercial interests in 1747 when his brother, Walter, died. Though he was certainly involved in the hat business, he is generally referred to as a 'Sugar Baker' or refiner, living in London, where he was sent to work as a young man.[15] This was probably after a short spell at Lincoln's Inn, where, as part of the typical education of the young gentleman of the period, he would have learned the rudiments of law, and gained the confidence to use the law to promote his own interests. He met his wife, Mary, in London society. She was the daughter of John Stiles of Uxbridge, and the couple appear to have spent more time in their London home in Lincoln's Inn Fields, than in Atherstone. Indeed, none of their children, Walter, Abraham or Elizabeth, were born in Atherstone.

In 1755 Abraham Bracebridge revived the issue which had brought his father close to ruin. He wrote to Michael Baxter, a lawyer and steward of the manor, saying that, 'a great number of the ables cottegers' (spelling was a congenital weakness in the Bracebridges) now had an 'earnest desire' for enclosure. He believed that the opportunity had now come, and that it was important to take it before, 'their present good opinion should be poizond by any Lover of Opposition'.[16] Although Abraham Bracebridge III, like his forbears, was quite capable of misrepresenting public opinion, there is no reason to disbelieve him in this case. The attitude towards enclosure was changing. Whilst in the period 1700–1760, nationally there had been only 152 acts of parliament to enclose the common fields, in

---

[14] Will of Abraham Bracebridge, 1692, CR258/229, and will of Walter Bracebridge, 1743, CR258/259, W.C.R.O.

[15] See the will of Samuel Bracebridge of Lindley, Co. Leics., Smyrna, 22 June 1767, PROB 12, 1146/466, Public Record Office.

[16] Letter from Bracebridge to Baxter, 8 August 1755, HR35/41, W.C.R.O.

the period 1761 to 1801 there were to be 1,479.[17] New farming methods favoured a diversity of crops, and selective breeding. This was difficult under the open field system. However, the cottagers of Atherstone were still opposed to enclosure, for as soon as they realised that Bracebridge wanted it, they began to think that there must be some disadvantage to themselves. The battle raged for several years, but by this time the advantages of enclosure were fully appreciated, and the cottagers did not have the backing of the freeholders. However, they persevered and in 1764, it was reported that they had raised £90 and were 'taking Measures to Oppose the Bill'.[18]

Supported by the majority of the freeholders, within a year an act had been passed to enclose the open fields. But to smooth the way, Abraham Bracebridge III had to resort to bribery. He offered to sell the lord of the manor's steward, Michael Baxter, a piece of land at a preferential price.[19] An agreement was made which Bracebridge did not honour, and Baxter eventually settled to buy the land at the market price, but used the situation to secure 100 acres for the use of the cottagers. This was grudgingly conceded by Bracebridge and raised the suspicions of the freeholders, who then marshalled opposition to the bill, believing that they would not receive adequate compensation for the land they were to lose.

Although this appears to have been no more than a threat, when the award was published in 1765, it can be seen that the land the freeholders was allotted is generally less than the area they owned under the open field system. For example, although Joseph Wilday did not live to receive his apportionment of land, his widow, Ann, was awarded a plot of one acre, two roods and fifteen perches, in the Innage, a field which lay behind their property in Long Street.[20] This was in lieu of three acres of meadow land, which Joseph had owned before enclosure. Either Joseph did not receive a fair exchange, or the lesser area represented better quality land, and was therefore equally as valuable as the area he had given up. In later years his family would appreciate the value of this piece of land, through which the Coventry Canal was cut, and on which in the 1820s they would build Atherstone's first gas works.

Meanwhile at Atherstone Hall, John Wilday, now in his thirties, was

---

[17] J. L. and B. Hammond, *The Village Labourer 1760–1832: A Study of the Government of England Before the Reform Bill* (First published London, 1911. Reprint 1987), p. 41.

[18] Report of meeting on 4 January 1764, HR35/51, W.C.R.O.

[19] Letter from Baxter to Bracebridge, 8 August 1764, HR35/49, W.C.R.O.

[20] Copy of enclosure award for Atherstone, 11 September 1765, W.C.R.O.

proving a sound manager for Bracebridge, looking after his interests in Atherstone and London. Bracebridge's marriage to Mary Stiles had extended his estate further. He now owned property in three other counties, Staffordshire, Hertfordshire and Middlesex, and had also inherited the family's former estates at Kingsbury and Hurley in Warwickshire. His house in Lincoln's Inn Fields was equipped with fine furniture, and his daughter, Elizabeth, would no doubt have been sufficiently proficient at the harpsichord to entertain influential visitors.[21] Bracebridge visited Atherstone only for business purposes, preferring to keep his family close to his wife's relations, and on visiting terms with London society, where they would be likely to make good marriages.

With enclosure now achieved and age overtaking him, it would be natural to assume that Abraham Bracebridge could now relax and enjoy the last years of his life in peace. But, this was not to be. Abraham Bracebridge III had one more goal to achieve before he died. This was the diversion of a road which ran a little too close to Atherstone Hall. The new road would be longer, less convenient, and would run though the narrow archway and yard of the Swan Inn in the market place. Stopping up the old road would also cut off access to property for some individuals.[22] The support of two local magistrates, one of whom, John Ludford, was a kinsman, should have been sufficient to ensure approval of the plan, but as in the first enclosure battle, Bracebridge had underestimated the power of local opposition. Led by the lord of the manor's agent, Dudley Baxter, they managed to defer the decision for eighteen months until the young lord of the manor, Charles Repington, reached his majority and was considered capable of making a decision. Much to Bracebridge's disgust, Repington refused to consent to the plan, and a compromise had to be made by modifying the route of the new road so that it did not run through the Swan Yard.

Whilst this battle was raging, Abraham's health began to fail, and he was looking for an excuse to ease himself out of the hatting trade. The major responsibility of the business had fallen on the capable shoulders of John Wilday, who had become a man of influence and wealth in his own right. Whilst the third partner, John Chapman, was primarily a banker, giving financial backing to the hat enterprise at Atherstone Hall, Wilday, a hatter, was the executive responsible for the day-to-day running of the business. Ideally he would have liked to become the sole owner,

---

[21] Will of Abraham Bracebridge 1789, CR258/259, W.C.R.O.

[22] Brief for the Respondents on an Appeal against an Order diverting a Certain part of an Highway in Atherstone, Warwick Easter Sessions, 8 April 1797, HR36, W.C.R.O.

and have authority to develop the trade as he saw fit. But under normal circumstances this was a vain hope, for the Bracebridges had always kept a tight hold on the reins. However, in 1774, his chance came unexpectedly. Abraham's younger son, Abraham, had become engaged to Mary Holte, the seventeen-year-old daughter of Sir Charles Holte of Aston Hall, near Birmingham. Here, at long last, was their opportunity to become fully accepted members of the Warwickshire gentry. The Holtes had owned the manors of Aston and Duddeston since the Middle Ages and had connections at Court, serving a succession of kings beginning with Henry VIII. In the civil war they had been ardent royalists, entertaining Charles I in 1642, and holding Aston Hall against a siege by the parliamentarians. Mary was the daughter of the sixth baronet, who had inherited the title from his brother, Sir Lister, who died without an heir. For the Brace-bridges, it was a brilliant marriage. The articles extend to several enormous parchments. A portion of £20,000 was agreed and a large sector of Atherstone property put into a trust for the benefit of Mary and her children. Every contingency was covered in the lengthy document, from protecting the interests of various permutations of unborn children, to provision for making the controversial new road.[23] In December 1774, as the wedding plans advanced, Bracebridge wrote to Mary's mother, Lady Ann Holte:

Atherstone Hall, Dec 6 1774

Dear Madam,

When I wrote the other day to Sir Chas I thought I might have had an oportunity of seeing him sooner than I now find it probable I may, or I shd have spoke of my intentions towards my son more particularly. The discourse I've had with him since makes me as anxious as himself to satisfy you in what manner the income, which I propose to allow him in present, will be secure to him in future; my concern in business has long been upon so permanent a foundation, that its certainty has been equal to its emolument, and cannot possibly, by any circumstance be prevented continuing so, as long as myself or successors think it worth their support.

The person to whom I now submit the management of it, has been with me many years, and has so sufficiently proved himself deserving the confidence that I have reposed in him that I have

---

[23] Minutes of Marriage Settlement, A. Bracebridge, Junior, and Mary Holte, 10 September 1775, CR258/212, W.C.R.O.

admitted him, to a small part as a partner that his care & diligence to me, might be further secured, by a proportionable benefit to himself which I considered more particularly necessary, till the attention & experience of my youngest son cd be sufficiently relyd on as an overseer, my infirm situation rendering my own attendance very uncertain but is now no otherways essential, than for our mutual convenience, for shd any circumstance happen to render it disagreable, the assistance of any other managers wd be readyly procured, & at a much less expence – and as the premises with a sufficient command of capital, will at my death become subject to the disposal of my eldest son, it will be totally in his own power to continue to himself the same advantages which are now injoy'd by me. I shd strongly recommend it to him to do so, as it need be no more trouble to him, than at present, & his property continued in trade wd be an advantage to his brother – but his discretion must be his guide; upon looking over the rents of my Estate here I find they at present amount to upwards of £900 per Annum – I never told my son more than £800 but that will be very soon advanced by a further benefit from the Inclosure, which I will make secure to him at my death. I will give my personal security to him for the payment of £1000 per Annum during my life, which I sometime ago promised him, so far independent of business as to be neither subject to uncertainty or attendance, and I shd hope the prudent part of life, which I may be considered to have taken may be thought a sufficient security for such a property at my death, as assisted by the above advantages he well knows will (as I have myself found it) be much more Valuable to him than his Estate.

It cannot be supposed that exclusive of my concern in trade and my Warwickshire Estate, I cd set apart from the rest of my famly such other property as wd give such an Income, but I shd hope the above will appear sufficiently satisfactory, for besides having my sons happyness much at heart, I shd myself be made exceedingly so, by seeing him so well settled.

I am with great regard to yourself & famly,
Yr most Obedient Humble Servant
Abraham Bracebridge [24]

---

[24] Letter from Abraham Bracebridge to Lady Mary Holte, 6 December, 1774, MR9/35, W.C.R.O.

It is unfortunate that Bracebridge did not mention John Wilday by name, but there can be little doubt that he is the 'person to whom I now submit the management'. His motives for giving John Wilday a small share of the business were clearly to secure his loyalty, perhaps in the face of Bracebridge's own enforced absence through illness. It is an indication of his acknowledgement of Wilday's commercial ability that he felt it necessary to discourage Wilday from leaving to set up a rival enterprise. But it was not in Bracebridge's nature to acknowledge Wilday's importance to him, and in professing that other managers could be found at 'much less expence' he was not being strictly honest with Lady Holte. The impression which he appears to be trying to convey is that Wilday was merely a temporary manager, who would step aside to allow Abraham Junior to take over, after he had served a sufficient apprenticeship. There is no suggestion that hatmaking was an inappropriate occupation for a gentleman. Indeed, the Holtes themselves had readily invested in ironworks in the past, and had shown no distaste for trade.[25]

A surprising aspect of this letter is Bracebridge's apparent confidence in the continued success of the business. His father had been in debt on his death, and his son was to suffer business failures too, though in soap rather than hats. The optimism was clearly intended to impress Sir Charles and Lady Holte, as to the solid basis of the Bracebridge finances. It seems that they were convinced, for the marriage took place, as planned, in September 1775. Within a year the couple's first child, Mary Holte, had been baptised in Mancetter Church.

No doubt John Wilday continued to manage the business at Atherstone Hall. He was approaching middle age and would have despaired of ever having the freedom to run things, as he, rather than Bracebridge, wished. But time was running out for the Bracebridges, for it appears that the optimism of 1774 was unfounded. Financial problems eventually forced Bracebridge to sell out to Wilday. It was not only the avid pursuit of land which ruined him, but also the expensive lifestyle with homes in London and Atherstone, and appearances to be maintained in society. Furthermore the Bracebridges' investments were not always sound, and their obsessive nature sometimes led to rash and ill-considered judgements. Although the date at which control passes to Wilday is unknown, by the time of Abraham Bracebridge III's death in 1789, the family had completely given up their interest in hatmaking.

At last, it appeared that the influence of the Bracebridges was on the

---

[25] M. B. Rowlands, *The West Midlands from AD 1000* (London, 1987), p. 146.

wane and they would never again exercise their power over local folk in pursuit of selfish ends. But no, Abraham Bracebridge IV was to show that he, too, had inherited the family's most characteristic gene. His father's plan to build the new road to divert passing traffic from the front of Atherstone Hall, had to be prosecuted. It was not a practical scheme for there was no suitable alternative route. This, however, was no impediment. Houses were pulled down and the road was routed through the archway and narrow yard of the Swan Inn, as planned. Today it remains a charming bottleneck in the road system, adding to the picturesque character of the market place, but too narrow to admit anything wider than single traffic.

The townsfolk watched these developments with some scepticism. Over generations they had learned to mistrust the Bracebridges' professed good intentions. Now they could not accept that the new scheme was of benefit to anyone but Bracebridge himself. They applied to the magistrates to view the new road before the old one was stopped up. Then, with Bracebridge's former agent, William Eborall, as their spokesman, the townsfolk objected to the stopping up. But Bracebridge had employed a good lawyer, who destroyed their case by questioning the motives of the individuals who had given support to Eborall.[26] The lawyer demolished all opposition by exposing a network of patronage and obligation, demonstrating that people had either misread the paper they were asked to sign, or signed because they did not wish to offend Mr Eborall. Many of these 'coerced' men were respected members of the community. Amongst them was John Wilday, who was forced to admit that he had only signed Mr Eborall's paper to return a favour, because Eborall had found employment for his son-in-law.

Why did these upright members of the community break their word under oath in a court of law? Were they threatened? It seems so, for the opposition crumbled away and Bracebridge achieved his objective. This case shows his isolation within the community. His erstwhile employees, tenants, and his father's two former partners, Chapman and Wilday, would only support him under threat. Eborall, his former agent, was, for a reason we do not know, set on a personal vendetta. One of those asked to sign the notice of appeal, a Mrs Moore, stated that Eborall told her, 'He should go to Gaol and be ruined if he did not beat Bracebridge in the Road Business'.[27] Perhaps this was his fate, for he is not heard of again.

---

[26] Watts & Winyard, p. 282.

[27] Brief for the Respondents on an Appeal against an Order diverting a Certain part of an Highway in Atherstone, Warwick Easter Sessions, 8 April 1797, HR36, W.C.R.O.

This case well shows that the Bracebridges, no longer local employers, could not with any reliability call upon any member of the community for support. Even John Wilday, nurtured under the Bracebridge wing, turned against them, once he had gained control of the hatting business, and no longer needed their patronage. The Bracebridges lived isolated,

10. Mary Bracebridge, wife of Abraham IV, and her daughter, Mary Holte, painted by George Romney between 1781 and 1784.

in Atherstone Hall and London, on the rents from their extensive property portfolio and their erratic business dealings.

Abraham Bracebridge IV and his wife, Mary, produced two daughters in the early years of their marriage. The charming portrait of Mary and her elder daughter, Mary Holte, by George Romney, left the family's possession early this century and appeared at various exhibitions in the U.S.A. In 1985 the painting came up for auction at Christie's in New York, and fortuitously, was bought by Birmingham Museums and Art Gallery, who have returned it to its rightful home at Aston Hall.

It seemed that Mary had inherited the Holtes' lack of success in producing heirs, until 1799, when, after twenty-four years of marriage, she gave birth to a son, Charles Holte, whilst staying with friends at Redland in Gloucestershire. Over the years the Holte family were to regret their daughter's choice of husband. Mary's mother, Lady Ann Holte, passed her widowhood at Atherstone Hall, but before she died in 1799, she tried hard to ensure that her son-in-law would not benefit from her death.[28] She would have watched with repressed anger as Abraham's business dealings went from bad to worse, but death spared her the ultimate humiliation which the Holtes were to suffer at his hands.

Abraham's wife, Mary, was in line to inherit the Holte estates as an heir general under the provision of the will of her uncle, Sir Lister Holte. In default of named heirs, the remainder of his estate was eventually to come to her. Abraham unwisely raised mortgages on the security of this reversion. He had invested in the soap business, and when it failed he was unable to meet his commitments. In 1817, to satisfy his creditors, he had to obtain an act of parliament to force the sale of the Holte estates. Two other heirs were still living, and under the act the proceeds were divided between them and Bracebridge's creditors. The contents of Aston Hall were auctioned and in 1818 the house passed into the hands of a firm of Warwick bankers, who leased it to the son of the engineer, James Watt. Then, in 1856, after his death, a fund was set up to buy the house and park as a place of recreation for the people of Birmingham. Charles Holte Bracebridge tried to make amends for his father's folly by presenting some of the remaining Holte family possessions to Birmingham City Council, which remains today the custodian of Aston Hall.

---

[28] Copy of the will of Dame Ann Holte, 3 November 1796, CR258/259, W.C.R.O.

CHAPTER 8

The Later Development
of the Hatting Trade

T HE LAST DECADE of the eighteenth century was a time of rapid
expansion for the Atherstone hatting trade. It may be ironical that
the boom came after the Bracebridges had sold out, but it was also poetic
justice, for the economic effect of enclosure was a major cause. Prior to
enclosure the cottagers were able to earn a reasonable living from their
generous rights of common, with hatmaking filling in the gaps in the
seasons when there was little work on the land. Afterwards, the cottagers
were dependent on the landowners for agricultural employment. It was
predicted during the campaign against enclosure of the 1730s that, 'The
Inferiour will be made slaves and oblig'd for what little work will be
found, to work for what those Mercenaries, who at present call them
Thieves, will please to give them.'[1] Despite Bracebridge's assurances to
the contrary, the prediction came true. The cottagers lost their independence, and became fully reliant on industrial occupation for their
livelihood.

This sudden availability of cheap labour could not have come at a more
convenient time for Wilday. Hatmaking has always prospered in times of
war, and the trade received a welcome boost during the 1770s when
Britain was at war with Spain and America, and cheap hats were needed
to equip the army. During the French wars the British army grew
considerably, until by the battle of Waterloo, it numbered 350,000 men,
all of whom required a hat.[2] There was also good business for Britain in
equipping enemy troops. Bonaparte's soldiers defeated the Russians in
1807 wearing British greatcoats, and a local tradition says that they marched
in stockings made in Hinckley.

It was basically the same hat, though shaped a little differently, which
equipped the British army, and the black slave as he laboured on the

---

[1] Cottagers answer to a paper entitled the 'Inclosure Vindicated', c.1738, HR35/15,
W.C.R.O.
[2] Asa Briggs, *The Age of Improvement: 1783–1867* (London, 1987), pp. 161–2.

West Indian and American plantations. Known as the 'billycock', this was a wool felt with an upturned brim. Serviceable in all weathers and cheap to make, it was the foundation of the Atherstone hat trade. The term derives from 'bully cock', first used in 1721 to describe a hat 'cocked after the fashion of the bullies or hectoring blades of the period.'[3] The billycock, or 'Atherstone Cock', was made from the eighteenth century onwards, and first worn by the army to quell the Young Pretender in 1745.[4] When Wilday took over Bracebridge's business, the hats became known as 'Wilday's Cocks', and when this contracted to 'billycock' it was erroneously claimed that Wilday had coined the term.

In later years another hatting family, the Veros, claimed the same distinction. When James Vero was on his death bed in 1898, he told his grandchildren that the billycock was made from 'Cock', or Italian, wool. He described it as having a round crown and curled brim, two to two-and-a-half inches in width, and weighing between four and five ounces. The hat was not dyed but had a narrow tape binding and a glazed cotton lining. In the early nineteenth century it sold for one shilling. James Vero claimed that 'They were afterwards nick named by the work people Billy Cocks from the fact that they were called cocks, and my grandfather's name being William who afterwards made them on his own account, hence were named after him as Billy Cocks'.[5]

This modest hat was the foundation of the Wilday fortunes in the early nineteenth century. Later the hatters would diversify, making a wide range of designs in various materials and qualities. However, the billycock was important to the trade because it could be made by men who were not fully skilled, and who may well have served incomplete apprenticeships. These were the men who came flocking into Atherstone in the last years of the eighteenth century to join the indigenous population who had lost their agricultural livelihood.

They came from hatmaking centres all over the country. Amongst them was John Vero who left the hatting town of Rugeley in Staffordshire, where his family still combined cottage feltmaking with agricultural labour. In his fifties, his father, also John, gave up hatting to become warrener to Sir Edward Littleton of Teddesley Hay on Cannock Chase.[6] John Vero

---

[3] Oxford English Dictionary.

[4] An article in *Umbrella and Portmanteau Trades' Review*, 1 December 1880, p. 609.

[5] Notes made from conversations with James Vero, 10 June 1895. Family papers in possession of the Executors of the late Mr A. B. T. Vero.

[6] Hatherton Estate Books, Teddesley Hay, Staffordshire: Day Books, 1752–1805, D260/M/E/27 – 28, Staffordshire Record Office.

was responsible for trapping rabbits and selling them at Wolverhampton market. At a shilling each, a rabbit would provide an adequate meal and a skin from which the fur could be shaved for 'plating' wool felt hats.[7] Whilst his two sons, William and John, were still feltmaking at home, John was able to supply them with the trimmings of fleeces, bought at fourpence a pound from Sir Edward, a pioneer of selective breeding.[8] When the sons were forced to leave home to look for work, they each went to separate hatting areas. William to Cheshire, and John to Atherstone.

Like Atherstone, Rugeley was a small market town which had been a hatting centre since the late seventeenth century. If any family could be said to have dominated the trade, it would probably have been the Salts, although the scale of their hatting enterprise was not on a par with the Bracebridges'. They were also local benefactors, who later founded the William Salt Library in Stafford.[9] Like Atherstone, Rugeley had a topography favourable to feltmaking. A water course flowed from Cannock Chase across the main street, giving the hatters easy access to soft water. Local coal mines provided fuel for the feltmaker's kettle, and the town, situated on the main Stafford to Lichfield road, had excellent communications. In 1818, Pitt remarked that, 'the principal manufacture is hats', but Rugeley was also an important centre for ironworking, and thus hatmaking never became as important an industry as it was in Atherstone.[10] In his *Directory* of 1834, White added 'sheet iron and cast iron material', to hats, as the town's principal manufactures, although at that time there were still thirty journeymen hatters working in the area.[11] After 1851 the trade began to decline.

John Vero would probably have been carrying his cancelled indentures to prove that he was a time-served man. Technically, he could have been said to be 'on the tramp'. This was the system adopted by out-of-work

---

[7] 'Plating' was the process whereby fur was made to adhere to a wool hat body, creating a hat with the luxurious feel of fur felt at a cheap price. It was later termed 'ruffing' and the men who carried out the process were known as 'ruffers'.

[8] Hatherton Estate Books: Day Book, 1752–1780, D260/M/E/27, S.R.O. An entry for 26 March, 1776, reads, 'Recd from John Verough for 28 lb of Birlings & Skirtings at 4*d.* per lb – 9*s.* 4*d.*'

[9] In probate material at L.J.R.O. the Salt family are recorded as feltmakers or hatters from 1692. James Salt who died in 1705/6 left household goods and hatting stock totalling £134 2*s.* 6*d.* See 'Rugeley Inventories 1640–1740', transcribed by D. C. M. Bramwell, L.J.R.O.

[10] W. Pitt, *Pitt's History of Staffordshire* (1817), p. 264.

[11] W. White, *History and Directory of Staffordshire* (1834), p. 508.

hatters, who were forced to travel from centre to centre in their search for work. At each town they would call at the turnhouse, an appointed place, usually an inn kept by a hatter. Here they would enquire if the town had any hatting work on offer. If so, one of the town's hatters would take the new arrival to the prospective employer and ask on his behalf. He was not allowed to tout for work himself.[12]

If there was no work the hatters had an obligation to pay relief to their comrades on the tramp. From 1816 when this system became more formalised, the hatters' emblem was shown on cards, issued as certificates of good character to men on the tramp. The motto, 'We assist each other in time of need' was a source of pride to the hatters and gave them some independence from the parish.[13] In fact, one of the difficulties in identifying the young hatters who came from elsewhere to settle in Atherstone is that there is no parish record of their arrival, no settlement certificate. All journeymen are said to have contributed to the local fund, probably at the rate of about two pence a week. It appears only to have been available to strangers on the tramp, because from 1819, when the parish vestry was formed in Atherstone, there are many cases of local out-of-work hatters applying for poor relief.[14]

The hatters' system of relief has been seen as forming 'a natural basis of trade union organisation'.[15] From as early as 1607, when the Feltmakers first received their royal charter, hatters had shown a strong tendency to combine. By 1771 there are records of local trade clubs existing in more than a dozen provincial towns, organised into a federation based on London.[16] There is evidence of trade union activity in Atherstone from 1817, showing that even though country areas might appear isolated from the larger hatting centres, they soon became part of a national organisation.[17]

John Vero, accompanied by his wife and child, arrived in Atherstone in 1786. He rented a small cottage and the use of a hatter's workshop at the east end of Long Street, from John Hincks, a woolcomber. Vero's work came from John Wilday, who had by this date established the beginnings of a hat factory at his home at the west end of Long Street.

---

[12] J. H. Smith, Chapter 4, p. 163.
[13] P. M. Giles, 'The Felt-Hatting Industry, c. 1500–1850 with particular reference to Lancashire and Cheshire', in *Transactions of the Lancashire and Cheshire Antiquarian Society*, LXIX (1959), p. 120.
[14] Atherstone Select Vestry Minute Book, 1819–1826, CR1130/13, W.C.R.O.
[15] Giles, p. 121.
[16] Giles, p. 122.
[17] Smith, Chapter 5, p. 235.

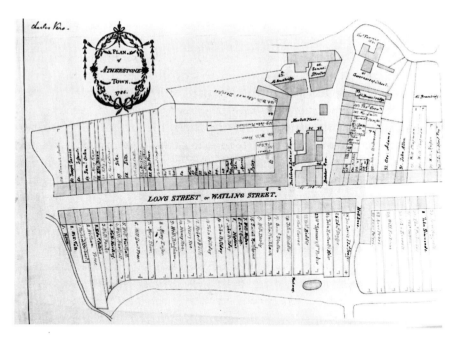

11. Detail of 'Plan of Atherstone Town' (1786), showing John Wilday's holding, and the Innage Brook to the west.

The expansion of the hat trade was beginning to have an effect on the shape of Atherstone. The houses on Long Street, the main thoroughfare, were set on long and narrow burgage plots which ran at right-angles to the street to parallel back roads on either side of Long Street, creating the plan of the classic 'street' town. At the west end of the town a brook ran along the 'Back Way'. During the late eighteenth century the burgages backing onto the brook were held by the town's tanners and dyers, but slowly the hatters displaced them and claimed for themselves the soft pure water essential to their trade.[18] The tanners and dyers let off the buildings in their yards to the incoming hatters. Later these buildings were replaced by rows of cottages on either side of the yard, which was narrow and unhealthy, on account of the open drain which ran along the centre. Eventually all but a few burgages in the town were filled up with tiny cottages and workshops, and as the years passed they became overcrowded and frequently visited by epidemics of typhoid, smallpox and scarlet fever.[19]

---

[18] Plan of Atherstone Town, 1786, CR2511/21, W.C.R.O.

[19] Watts & Winyard, p. 192.

At that time, there was no question of extending the town and building on greenfield sites because neither of the two major landowning families, the Bracebridges and the Dugdales, would give up any of their expansive acres to relieve the housing problem. The Dugdales, as lords of the manor, owned land immediately to the south in the neighbouring parish of Merevale, and also much of the main street property. The latter was mainly held by tenants as copyhold, and carried with it the obligation to pay dues to the lord of the manor. Even the Bracebridges could not escape this, and their name frequently appears amongst the lists of defaulters. The Bracebridges had consolidated their own landholding since enclosure and owned the freehold of most of the land to the north of the main street, with some property in the town centre. As landlords they were able to profit from the hatting boom by renting out cottages and workshops, but it was trifling by comparison with Wilday's bonanza.

From the time he took over from Bracebridge, John Wilday was an innovator. In Leathermills Lane, Hartshill, where, in the seventeenth century, Samuel Butler had established the parish's first major feltmaking shop, in the 1790s Wilday erected its first powered carding machine.[20] With a water wheel providing the main power it could prepare large quantities of wool, which was then transported in sacks the mile or so to Atherstone, for putting out to the feltmakers. It may well be said that Wilday, in using water power when steam was available, could hardly be at the forefront of technology. However, the water wheel was cheap and easy to install, and recent modifications to its design had allowed it to come into its own for industrial purposes well after the steam engine had become firmly established.[21]

By 1796 many of the hatting processes had been brought in-house, under one roof, as specialised premises were developed. One hatmaker, Mrs Ann Power, who had inherited her husband's business and was running it with her son, John, had the beginnings of a factory at this time. She had a 'Bason shop', where the wool received its initial compacting (or hardening). The next stage, feltmaking (or planking) was still put out. The hood came back to be dried in the 'Stove', then brushed with proof in the 'Stiffening Shop'. It was then blocked and dyed in the 'Dyehouse', before being shaved and polished in one of the '5 Finishing shops'.[22] Finally the hat was put out again for trimming, before returning to one of Mrs Power's two warehouses prior to despatch.

---

[20] Order Book of the New Fire Office, 1784–1799, CR1039/1, W.C.R.O.

[21] Neil Cossons, *The BP Book of Industrial Archaeology* (Newton Abbot, 1987), pp. 47–8.

[22] Order Book of the New Fire Office, 1784–1799, CR1039/1, W.C.R.O.

12. A planking shop in the 1840s.

By 1803 another hatter, Edmund Simonds, had installed a horse-powered carding machine on his premises in the main street.[23] Although a planking shop is included too, for the use of Simonds himself, he also has two other planking shops, both rented out to independent hatters, who lived in adjoining tenements. Some of the buildings were thatched and the yard also included stables. Often there were pigsties and cowhouses too.

The most common system amongst country feltmakers in the late eighteenth century, and the method which Bracebridge and Wilday appear to have adopted, was for the master to weigh out the wool on his premises, then put out the bowing, basoning and planking at piece rates, bringing the work back in house for stiffening, dyeing and finishing.[24]

The men would visit the warehouse and collect their wool in large

[23] Phoenix Fire Office of London, 1790–1803, CR1039/2, W.C.R.O.
[24] J. H. Smith, Chapter 4, p. 152.

bags known as 'padding pokes' which they carried home slung over their shoulders.[25] Whereas in the seventeenth century the cottage had been the only workplace, with one of its very few rooms given up to the trade, by the eighteenth century the workshop had become an addition to the house, and was a place where several men could work communally.

There was nothing of the clinical mass production of the modern factory in the craft of feltmaking. Wool, a natural substance, was subjected to the elements of nature, namely fire and water, to transform it into felt. The steamy smell of the felt shop was as earthy as the atmosphere of the stable next door. The term 'Mystery' was used by the old Livery Company to describe the art of feltmaking. This was, in fact, a corruption of 'mastery'. But 'mystery' well expresses that strange and almost mystic transformation of wool into felt which happened under the calloused and rough hands of the feltmaker.

When the felt was made, hoods would be piled in the yard, and left outside to dampen so that they were ready for blocking. Urine was collected from the stables and houses to add alkali to the dye. To add to the variety of odours, there was often a pig in the yard, which recycled household waste and provided the occupants with a seasonal feast. The ritual of slaughter, performed by a visiting butcher, who brought his own pig bench, was a sight for everyone, young and old. The hatters worked amidst the daily routine of the yard, watched by their children and helped by their wives. The small masters in their independent shops nearby supplemented the needs of the large masters, who provided the carded wool, organised the various processes and finally distributed the finished hats. The large master kept an account book in which he recorded the production of the small master and paid him his dues weekly.[26] Out of his income the small master would need to give his apprentice a small remuneration.

Apprentices were generally bound for a period of seven years. Out of eighty-five hatting apprentices recorded in Warwickshire for the period 1700 to 1834, fifty-four were from Atherstone.[27] Fifty-two of the total eighty-five were apprenticed for seven years, and eighteen for longer terms. A high proportion of these children were poor and dependent on charity. It has been suggested that this was because it was a dirty trade.

[25] J. H. Smith, Chapter 4, p. 165.

[26] Vero & Everitt Wages Book, 1855–1857. Family papers in possession of the Executors of the late Mr A. B. T. Vero.

[27] Joan Lane, 'Apprenticeship in Warwickshire, 1700–1834', Ph.D. thesis, University of Birmingham, 1977, p. 401.

However, the numbers include enough sons of the more prominent tradesmen and master hatters for this to be not altogether a fair criticism.

In 1794, hatter John Purkins, took thirteen-year-old John Hawkesford, a 'poor Child' of Coleshill, apprentice for eight years, on the understanding that he provide 'sufficient Meat, Drink, Apparel, Lodging, Washing & other Things necessary & fit for an apprentice'.[28] Unhappily the relationship was not successful for John Hawkesford was soon 'set out afresh by his father' and went on to serve another master.

Since 1776 the laws on apprenticeship had been relaxed. Previously a master was allowed to take only two apprentices, but following the repeal of the act, he was allowed as many apprentices as time-served journeymen. The problem in some areas was finding enough journeymen who had served the full seven year apprenticeship themselves.[29] As a relatively remote country area, it would be natural to assume that the feltmakers of Atherstone paid scant heed to the directions of parliament, but although this might have been so in the seventeenth century, by the late eighteenth century it appears that most were working within the law.

As businesses grew, particularly at the time of the American wars, the master hatters began to seek ways of improving efficiency, and to minimise loss through embezzlement and shrinkage. Bringing the processes in-house was an effective way of eliminating this. Furthermore, selling to the armed forces would require the presence of an agent in London, who could deal with the many pitfalls in dealing with government procurement agencies. Thus, gradually the Atherstone trade evolved into the large industry it would become by the turn of the century. However, it never seriously overcame the prejudices of hatters in other parts of the country, who maintained a superior attitude towards the country trade. In the early 1800s it was said of the Atherstone trade that, 'If a man dropped a hat from his pad on coming down from the bow garret, he would rather than pick it up go back and bow and basin another'.[30]

In 1809 John Wilday died and was succeeded by his son, Joseph, aged twenty-three. Joseph Wilday set up the first purpose-built factory for feltmaking. Indeed, in a trade where expansion of premises was usually piecemeal and caused by the needs of the moment rather than the grand design of the architect, model factories were almost unknown. In 1814, still under thirty, he was showing how far ahead the trade had come

---

[28] Atherstone Parish Apprenticeship Records, 10 December 1794, DR(B)100/108/95, W.C.R.O.
[29] J. H. Smith, Chapter 4, p. 151.
[30] J. H. Smith, Chapter 4, p. 162.

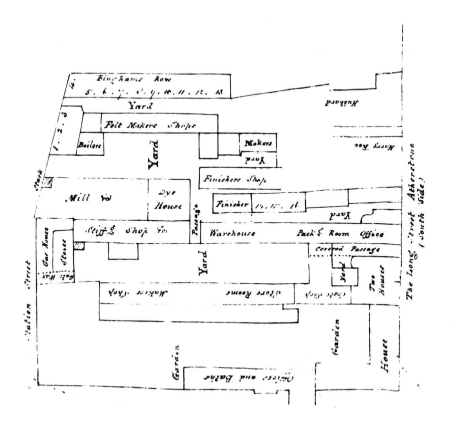

13. Plan of Wilday's model factory as it remained in 1861 when Hall and Phillips leased the premises.

under his control. Still on the same site, fronting the main street, Wilday's house contained his offices and bank. All processes following the planking had now been brought in-house.[31] Wilday had a room for making white hats, which had to be kept scrupulously clean. A year or so later, 'damping shops' had been built, to prepare the hoods for blocking, rather than leaving them out to weather in the yard. By 1826 a steam boiler had been installed to provide the copious amounts of steam needed to harden wool and shape hats.

Then, in a surprising move, in 1834 Wilday handed over the hatting and banking business to a partnership from Rugeley by the name of Weaver and Walsh. The reason for this is obscure, although there was a

---

[31] Phoenix Fire Office, 1811–1831, CR1039/4, W.C.R.O.

family connection, since, in 1804, Charles Weaver had married Joseph's sister, Susan. However, in February 1834, shortly before Weaver and Walsh took over, there had been a turnout of hatters working for Wilday in Atherstone. This was part of a national action following a congress in Liverpool where wage rates and apprentice numbers had become matters of contention. In Atherstone the trade was already suffering a setback following the abolition of slavery in 1807. By 1833 the slaves had been freed and did not wish to wear cheap Atherstone hats. As it was said at the time, 'Emancipation has given them more refined notions'.[32]

The hatters applied to the parish vestry for poor relief because, as it appears, they could not get benefit from their union. Many found themselves in fear of the union which had put them in a cruel dilemma at a difficult time. On the one hand they wished to show solidarity with their fellow workers in the fight for better rates, but on the other they had their families to consider. Ambrose Horton, a hatter journeyman with a wife and six children, approached the parish vestry saying that he 'Could not take out work if Mr Willday would give him any'.[33] But once the hatters had turned out, Wilday made it clear that he would not allow them back to work unless it was on his terms.

John Archer (alias Fearfield, a hatter and a piecemaster), told the parish vestry that Wilday had refused to give him work, 'Last Thursday Week, the day he took in his pad. The foreman booked him no more Work and he did not ask him for any Work at that time nor (had) he asked for any since.' Feltmakers, John Chinn and James Hogg, told the vestry that on the previous Wednesday week they had taken in their completed pad. But after the hats had been looked over, and presumably found acceptable, Mr Bailey, Wilday's foreman, had told them that there was no more work at present. Another feltmaker, Thomas Cooper, also took in his work, but had seen Wilday, who said to him, 'I wish you to tell your fellow Workmen that so long as you continue in this Tomfools Union I can do nothing for you, but if you wish to withdraw yourselves from it I will be a Friend to them'. He added that Wilday also told him that the men interfered in many things and prevented him from taking an apprentice. This was another reason for the turnout, for although the rule allowing a master to take no more than two apprentices had been relaxed, the unions had called for its return. Apprentices could be regarded as cheap labour, for the apprentice was only paid a small amount from his master's

---

[32] *Post Office Directory of Warwickshire* (1845), p. 593.
[33] Atherstone Select Vestry Minute Book, 1828–36, CR3056/1, W.C.R.O.

own pocket. A bright and eager boy could quickly become a considerable moneyspinner to his master who took the boy's work as his own.

Whether industrial unrest was a cause of Wilday passing over his business to Weaver and Walsh in summer 1834 remains uncertain, for it is likely that Rugeley was similarly affected. The partnership had a large premises in Rugeley, where most of the finishing processes were undertaken, suggesting that the feltmaking was still being put out, as it was in Atherstone. Their Rugeley factory included a blocking, a stiffening, and a colouring shop, a stove and several warehouses.[34]

During the 1830s some Atherstone hatters were forced to leave their families in the town whilst they went off to other hatting centres to look for work. Some went to Rugeley, and may have gone to work for Weaver and Walsh thus strengthening the link between the two hatting centres which had begun with John Vero's arrival in 1786. Weaver and Walsh modernised the Atherstone trade considerably, installing steam engines and gas, and acquiring additional premises at the former Pinchback's Mill beside the Coventry Canal, where today, the last surviving wool felt hat factory in Atherstone, Wilson & Stafford, still stands. A new innovation was the installation of a blowing machine which enabled them to make fur felt bodies. Unlike modern wool felt forming, where a web of carded wool is wound on to a revolving cone, to make fur felt the shaved fur is blown on to a metal cone. The fur 'batt' requires very gentle treatment during its initial hardening, but results in a fine and expensive hat. Despite their innovations, Weaver and Walsh did not enjoy the success they sought, for trade was still dull. It was probably during this time that the practice developed of spending the slack winter period underground digging coal. Summer layoffs were not such a problem as there was usually work in haymaking, often on the master's own land. There are several entries in the wage books to show that hatters were able to turn their hand to this and other tasks, including building when the factories required extension.

After 1838 John Weaver passed the hatmaking back to Joseph Wilday and concentrated on his banking business. Following a fire in 1841, Wilday built his model factory, expanding into 'fine hats', and impressing his insurance agent with the quality of the building. 'From the manner which the fireplaces are made & secured by the brick and Iron hearths I am of the opinion that there is no more danger that a fire would take place than from a common fireplace in a room.'[35] The use of resins for stiffening

---

[34] Phoenix Fire Office Order Book, 1834–52, CR1039/5, W.C.R.O.
[35] Phoenix Fire Office Order Book, 1834–52, CR1039/5, W.C.R.O.

felt and making pith helmets created a serious fire hazard, which the hatters were at pains to minimise, and which the insurance companies paid particular attention to, when they were assessing risk.

During the mid-nineteenth century, well after other industries, the hatting industry began to look seriously at mechanisation. Intelligent employees, as well as masters, patented inventions which they hoped would enable hats to be made more quickly and cheaply than by the manual method. Industrial espionage was rife and employers went to great lengths to protect their ideas. In Stockport in 1851, William Barber, an employee of Christy & Company, invented a press to shape the billycock. In his memoirs he wrote:

> We did all we could to keep the thing secret. The press-room was always apart or partitioned off from the others. Once it was in the kitchen, another time it was in the shaping shop. Once I went for Moulds to Coalbrookdale for the sake of excellence and secrecy . . . In spite of all our care the particulars of the machine were literally stolen.[36]

The forming machine was in use by the 1830s, superseding the old bowing method of preparing wool batts.[37] Other inventions were imported from America, where there was a thriving hat industry, based on Philadelphia. There John B. Stetson began to make his famous hat in the mid-nineteenth century. In the 1860s machines had been imported from America to replace the basoning and planking stages of hatmaking. The 'jigger' was used to press the formed wool between vibrating surfaces made hot and damp by the introduction of steam. The planking machine or 'barrel twister', as it was more commonly known, replaced the manual working of the wool with a series of rollers through which the body was rolled and twisted until it felted. Another 'innovation' introduced from America was the use of the old Yorkshire fulling mill, or stock, to felt the hat body.[38] The dampened bodies were placed in the trough and pounded by the oak hammers until the wool felted (see illustration 3, page 12). Although the barrel twister has now been superseded by beds of multi-rollers, the other hat machines are still in use today. Indeed, the slow nature of the felting process with its many different stages has been

---

[36] W. Barber, *The Chronicles of Canal Street from Before Christys to 1868*, ed. J. Christie-Miller (Stockport, 1965), p. 23.
[37] A. Ure, *The Philosophy of Manufactures of the Factory System of Great Britain*, first edition, 1835 (London, 1967), p. 191.
[38] Barber, p. 29.

resistant to innovation, and, though many have tried, no-one in the world has yet succeeded in fully mechanising the manufacture of a wool felt hat.

The new machinery was slow to come to Atherstone. Labour was cheap and there was little incentive to invest large sums of money in plant and equipment. New factories were hurriedly and poorly built, as and when circumstances permitted. Consequently few have survived. The masters were conscious of every penny they spent. Down to the last farthing everything was meticulously accounted for, and, as was to be expected, they drove a hard bargain over rates. In times of layoff there was great poverty amongst the hatters and the parish vestry books are full of their appeals for poor relief.

Joseph Wilday, as a member of the parish vestry, was often delegated with the task of finding work for an applicant. A bachelor of ascetic habit, he insisted on prayers being read every day before work in his factory. He was said also to have read the bible to inmates of the town's workhouse. He insisted on cleanliness and order, encouraging his employees to take a pride in their craft. Although he clearly modelled himself on the philanthropic textile barons of the north, Wilday was not a popular employer. As a former employee wrote in 1890, 'Mr Wilday was in some respects a kind man, but he was a tyrant also, and kicked and cuffed men . . .'[39] When he died in October 1852, there was little grieving for Joseph Wilday. William Vero, a master hatter, wrote to his son in Australia:

> You will be surprised, but not sorry to hear that my old and unflinching enemy, Mr Jos Willday, Hatter, died at 7 o'clock tonight. I was just going past his House, when they brought the news out. He has made me suffer much by his life . . . He was ill about a week [with] desese stoppage in the water.[40]

The autocracy which the Bracebridges had imposed on the local people was carried on by their economic heirs. But, whilst Wilday abused his employees, the local people had forgotten how the Bracebridges had previously abused them. In the mid-nineteenth century this family was still the local symbol of respect and power, residing in Atherstone Hall, a stone's throw from the market place. But now the Bracebridges, no longer economically involved in the town's business affairs, were free to

---

[39] Watts and Winyard, p. 325, quoted from 'Atherstone News', 24 January 1890.
[40] Vero family papers: Letters between William and Lettice Vero, et al., and Charles Vero and James Everitt, 1852–1855, 27 October 1852.

become champions of the people. Charles Holte Bracebridge was a committed Liberal. People turned to him for advice and financial assistance in times of need. In him there was never a hint of the cruel role which his ancestors had played in local life.

14. Charles Holte Bracebridge, 1864.

CHAPTER 9

Charles Holte Bracebridge: The Hatters' Friend

H E WAS: 'A man nearly sixty, of acquiescent temper, miscellaneous opinions, and uncertain vote. He had travelled in his younger years, and was held in this part of the county to have contracted a too rambling habit of mind. (His) conclusions were as difficult to predict as the weather: It was only safe to say that he would act with benevolent intentions, and that he would spend as little money as possible in carrying them out.'[1]

Mr Brooke, a character in George Eliot's fictional portrait of Midland life, *Middlemarch*, published in 1871, was almost certainly based upon Charles Holte Bracebridge, described by Eliot's biographer as, 'a muddle-headed magistrate of Atherstone', who, in the 1850s, was the cause of much anguish to the novelist.[2] Throughout his life Bracebridge was a dabbler, concerning himself with issues he did not always fully understand. He achieved national fame when he and his wife, Selina, accompanied Florence Nightingale to the Crimea, but even that, most brave of gestures, did not enhance his reputation.

Charles Holte Bracebridge was born in 1799 to middle-aged parents, who had long despaired of producing a son. His father, Abraham, captain of the parish infantry, led a voluntary contingent of between ninety and one hundred 'well-known tradesmen and business men of the town' in the Napoleonic Wars.[3] There is no record of any deed of daring of these forerunners of the Home Guard, but they were splendidly dressed in cocked hats, white breeches and long black gaiters.

Abraham had also found time to rebuild Atherstone Hall, hardly more than a hundred years after its previous rebuilding. With the disputed new road now laid through the narrow yard of the Swan Inn, the hall was distanced from the town, in which burgage plots were burgeoning with tenements of increasingly poor quality. The end of the Napoleonic War

---

[1] George Eliot, *Middlemarch*, ed. W. J. Harvey (Middlesex, 1979), p. 30.
[2] G. S. Haight, *George Eliot: A Biography* (Oxford, 1968), p. 284.
[3] Watts and Winyard, p. 278.

brought a slump in the hatting trade, and the many men who had flocked into the town during the late years of the eighteenth century were forced to turn to the parish vestry for help. John Vero, who had come to Atherstone so optimistically in 1786, was an old man in December 1819, begging the vestry for 'work or relief'.[4] Charles Holte Bracebridge, grew to manhood during these years of hardship. His experience of the sufferings of the local community led to the development of a social conscience and made him a pioneering spirit in the field of social and penal reform.[5]

From his youth he exhibited the eclecticism which would earn him the reputation of a 'dabbler'. His commonplace book contains cuttings and quotations from a bizarre range of interests. Juxtaposed with an analysis of the mineral waters of Moira, Warwick and Kenilworth, are snippets from Shakespeare and astronomy. The suggestion that his taste might have bordered on the perverse is found in a description of a Hindu woman's act of suttee, and a caution to ladies on the dangers of wearing revealing dresses.[6]

Bracebridge did not participate in the usual country pursuits of a gentlemen, but occupied himself with trying to improve the life of the poor. Like Mr Brooke in *Middlemarch*, he was a passionate advocate of parliamentary reform, and like him too, he tried unsuccessfully to get into parliament. As a Liberal candidate, he stood for the northern division of Warwickshire, in the elections of 1837.[7] Then in later life he contested the seat for Tamworth. His election address of 1863 appeals to the voter's social conscience, 'I Have humbly but earnestly supported the cause of Education, Sanitary Reform, and other measures illustrating in our age the sympathy existing between all classes of our countrymen.' This was not an empty claim; Bracebridge had given the land, the buildings and an endowment to enable a new school to be opened in Atherstone. Afterwards, the school log recorded his frequent visits. In his role as a magistrate he was able to investigate the work of the poor law guardians, but also spent money from his own pocket to help the needy. Bracebridge was a founder member of the Social Science Association, and contributed several papers, though none appear to have been received with any enthusiasm by the theorists of the day.

Bracebridge never became an accepted member of the humanitarian establishment, although he numbered Harriet Martineau, the social

---

[4] Atherstone Vestry Minute Book, 1818–1868, DR322/59, W.C.R.O.

[5] See J. Saunders, 'Warwickshire Magistrates and Prison Reform, 1840–75', *Midland History*, Vol. XI (1986).

[6] Commonplace Book, undated but post-1820, CR258/479, W.C.R.O.

[7] Saunders, p. 88.

campaigner, amongst his circle of friends. She, too, was the child of an unsuccessful sugar refiner, and in 1845 whilst recuperating from an illness, was invited to Atherstone Hall, where the Bracebridges introduced her to George Eliot. It was a friendship which would last for life. Bracebridge had known Eliot since her childhood, for her father, Robert Evans, had once been his land agent, and she would have first come to Atherstone Hall accompanying her father on his business.[8]

Bracebridge's introduction to Harriet Martineau, whose circle included many of the leading radicals of the day, was through his wife, Selina. She has been described as 'a remarkable woman, beautiful in a regal style . . . intellectual, artistic and possessing an extraordinary warmth of character'.[9] She was born, Selina Mills, of Hill Street, Berkeley Square, London, and brought a fortune of £18,000 to her marriage in 1824. In 1846 Selina met Florence Nightingale, twenty years her junior, and remained her close friend for the rest of her life. It was almost a mother and daughter relationship, for Selina was denied children of her own and poured upon Florence all her unsatisfied maternal feeling. Nightingale's biographer, Cecil Woodham-Smith, believed that Selina's importance to Florence was 'overwhelming'.[10] Nightingale left notes in which she revealed her full dependence on Selina. She imagined that Selina was always with her and wrote fanciful dialogues about their relationship which she was too embarrassed to show to her friend.

Selina was a woman of charisma and intelligence, who attracted and influenced one of the most remarkable women of all time. Her husband, though generous and well-meaning, was no match for her. Some of his actions were rash and ill-considered, and no doubt he was occasionally an embarrassment to his wife, though she never reproached him. It was said that the Bracebridges were very happily married, and it is evident in his writings that Bracebridge tried hard to become his wife's intellectual equal. In addition to social problems, he interested himself in cultural matters. As secretary of the Shakespeare House Committee, he raised funds for what would later become the Birthplace Trust, and produced an inconsequential paper on the famous deer-stealing incident. He trawled the plays for all references to hunting and gamekeeping and put forward a new view, which has found little favour with posterity. His thesis that the deer-stealing incident took place at Fulbroke, rather than Charlecote

---

[8] Saunders, p. 98.
[9] C. Woodham-Smith, *Florence Nightingale, 1820–1910* (London, 1950), p. 66.
[10] Woodham-Smith, p. 67.

has added little to Shakespeare research and only confirms Bracebridge's reputation as a dabbler.[11]

The Bracebridges were great travellers and filled the vacuum of their childlessness with long journeys, especially to Greece, for which Selina had a particular love. They owned property in Athens and, characteristically, Bracebridge showed his firm support for the freedom of the Greek people by participating in their revolt against the Turks. His passion for liberty was emphasised by his picturesque dress of wide hats and flowing cloaks, and also by the spirited Arab horses which he imported from the East and bred at Atherstone Hall.[12] Sometimes the Bracebridges took Florence with them on their travels. In the winter of 1847, whilst she was recovering from one of her frequent emotional breakdowns, they took her to Italy, the country of her birth. Dancing through the midnight hours, Florence enjoyed what she later described as the happiest New Year of her life.[13] Two years later they travelled to Egypt.

In Atherstone in 1853, the hatters were giving Bracebridge cause for concern. Since the 1840s, when the full effects of the abolition of slavery had finally seeped through to Atherstone, there had been a general slump nationally in the feltmaking trade, resulting in much undercutting by masters in other parts of the country. Inevitably the attention turned to Atherstone, where in 1848 the partners of the Stockport firm, Christy and Company, sent industrial spies to find out how hats could be made so cheaply.[14] The answer was simple. The Atherstone feltmakers were making hats at prices which would barely allow them to keep body and soul together. Many gave up hatmaking and, seduced by the possibility of instant wealth, joined the gold rush to Australia. Others cautiously wondered if it was possible to expand the hat industry to Australia. Amongst them were two Atherstone men, Charles Vero, a hatter, and James Everitt, by trade a tallow chandler.

Bracebridge lent them £80 to pay their fare on the hazardous voyage to Australia. They did not prosper as they hoped, for times were hard in Australia too. Letters from home refer to 'Mr Bracebridge's interest' in their progress, and are full of reminders of the debt owed to him and to

---

[11] C. Holte Bracebridge, 'Shakespeare No Deerstalker, or A Short Account of Fulbroke Park, Near Stratford on Avon' (London, 1862).
[12] Woodham-Smith, p. 66.
[13] Woodham-Smith, p. 69.
[14] J. H. Smith, Chapter 4, p. 186.

other creditors.[15] William Vero, master hatter and keeper of the town's lock-up, was unable to rest until the money was repaid. Eventually the cash was scraped together and, on March 20th 1854, a banker's order for £140 arrived in the post from Melbourne. William was anxious to repay the £80 to Bracebridge as soon as possible. The following day, accompanied by his son, James, who carried some hats made in Melbourne and a map of the town (to show exactly where the Everitt & Vero shop was situated), William went up to Atherstone Hall.

He found Bracebridge relaxed and in good spirits, having just returned from one of his frequent trips to Italy. Having listened to the report of Everitt & Vero's progress, he expressed himself 'much pleased' to hear how well they were coping in Australia, and promised to cash the money order without 'a farthing expense' to them. William, being also the lord of the manor's bailiff and town constable, considered himself to be a man of honour. Nevertheless, when times were so hard it was difficult parting with money and he knew that the balance of £60 was desperately needed by his family. It seems that William and his son were unable to disguise these sentiments, for Bracebridge noticed the pain in the men's eyes as they stood before him, cap in hand, wishing, but not daring to ask, if Bracebridge could cash the order quickly, as the money was needed to finance the making of a few more hats to send out to Australia for Everitt & Vero to sell.

Bracebridge was in some ways a sensitive man. He smiled at them and said gently, 'You want the £60, do you not?' William straightened himself and mustered his dignity, '*I* do not want it as I have got plenty of money, but I would like this son of mine to have it, to make goods for Australia.'

'I do not want the £80', Bracebridge replied, as if intending to forgo his loan. He offered to cash the money order in London in a few days. This gave the hard-pressed hatters a little more breathing space. However, a month later William and James were still waiting for the money. William wrote to Melbourne, 'Dear Children . . . I have not heard from the Victoria Bank Order, but Mr Bracebridge is gone to London. Shall have something when he comes Back'.

Unbeknown to Vero, Bracebridge had weightier matters on his mind. War had broken out in the Crimea. In fact, that very day, April 26th, 1854, had been appointed by Queen Victoria as a day of 'National humiliation and prayer, for the success of the war, in which we are now

---

[15] Letters between William and Lettice Vero, *et al.*, and Charles Vero and James Everitt, in Melbourne, 1852–1855. Vero Family Papers in possession of the Executors of the late Mr A. B. T. Vero.

ingaged with Russia'. That summer was disastrous for the British troops, their numbers decimated, not by the Russian army, but by cholera which had struck a thousand of them by September.

Wars have usually been good for the hat trade, and indeed during this period, England in general was enjoying a time of economic wellbeing. But, although the hatters of Atherstone read of prosperity in the newspapers, they enjoyed none of it themselves.[16] The market for cheap felts with wide brims, suitable for keeping the sun off, 'thrashers' as they were termed, had been briefly boosted by the Australian trade in 1853, but by 1854 decline had set in. It was the worst spring in living memory, with feltmakers and finishers on three days work at most. Some, as it was reported to Melbourne, 'were actually dying of starvation and going mad with anxiety'.

Bracebridge, though preoccupied with Florence Nightingale and the war, returned to Atherstone in July for the annual general meeting of the town's Literary Institution. Then, in October, he and Selina set off with Florence Nightingale on their historic journey to the Crimea.[17] The scenes of squalor, deprivation and death which met them in Scutari are well documented, and it is to the Bracebridges' credit that they adapted well to a hideous situation made worse by bureaucracy and a refusal of the military authorities there to co-operate. Occasionally Bracebridge's temper could not be curbed, and this led to further difficulties for Florence Nightingale, whose health broke down under the strain. She had hardly recovered when the Bracebridges told her that they wished to return home.

> They had come to the end of their endurance. For nine months they had shared the fearful sights, the horrible smells, the uneatable food, the insolence, the petty slights and the perpetual rudeness. They had endured, toiled, sacrificed themselves and yet – they had not been a complete success. Their devotion was as strong as ever, Miss Nightingale's affection as grateful. "No one can tell what she has been to me", she wrote of Selina, but Selina had muddled the "Free Gift" store, and Mr Bracebridge's relations with the officials were increasingly unhappy.[18]

Although she was sad to see them go, in her heart of hearts Florence must have been relieved. She soon discovered that it was easier to get on

---

[16] Letter from L. and M. Vero in Atherstone, to James and Sarah Everitt, 1 June, 1854. Vero Family Papers.
[17] Woodham-Smith, p. 142.
[18] Woodham-Smith, p. 224.

without Mr Bracebridge to hinder her. But, ironically, even then she could not escape from his interference. In September 1855, he and Selina made a much publicised triumphal return to Atherstone, accompanied by Florence's sister, Parthe. The following month Bracebridge gave a lecture in Coventry, attacking the British army authorities and doctors. Many of his allegations were unsubstantiated, and when Florence received a copy of *The Times'* report of the lecture, she was devastated. All her efforts in building up a working relationship with the authorities were wasted. In a few ill-chosen words Bracebridge had destroyed everything she had worked for. She had to begin again.

The war was still proving a mixed blessing to the hatters of Atherstone. It was reported that Hall & Phillips, who had bought Joseph Wilday's business after his death, had a 'large order for the army'.[19] And in the same letter, 'The war is the cry and I can tell you, it is serious. We have lost a good many Atherstone Chaps. May we soon be blessed with peace.' In March, 'We have been forced to live on Bacon because we have no money to buy anything with.' Charles Vero, unable to stand the climate had returned from Australia, and was attempting to establish a hat manufactory in Atherstone. 'The war makes the Soldiers' Cap trade good', he wrote to James Everitt in Melbourne, 'A Gentleman came and offered me unlimited orders, but I was short of two requisites, men and money. I scraped £8 15s. 6d. to send for one description of wool, and Wilson trusted me with £13 4s. 0d. of another sort and I have taken an order of 1000, 300 of which I have nearly completed, working all hours myself at dyeing and all the disagreeable work.'[20]

The war ended in March 1856 at a cost of 22,000 lives and fifty million pounds. Florence Nightingale continued her campaign for hospital reform, and Selina Bracebridge remained her close friend. It was not long, however, before Charles Holte Bracebridge was meddling again. When the novelist George Eliot's first works of fiction were published under this pseudonym, there was great speculation about the true identity of the writer. A Nuneaton man, Joseph Liggins, claimed that he had written the books. This provoked a long debate in the press in 1858, to which Bracebridge contributed energetically. But, when it was finally discovered that Liggins was not the writer, Bracebridge refused to accept the fact, and insisted that, if Liggins had not actually written the books, then he

---

[19] Letters between William and Lettice Vero, *et al.*, and Charles Vero and James Everitt, in Melbourne, 1852–1855. Vero Family Papers.
[20] Letters between William and Lettice Vero, *et al.*, and Charles Vero and James Everitt, in Melbourne, 1852–1855. Vero Family Papers.

must have provided the material. Bracebridge's letters, written to George Eliot's friends, Charles and Cara Bray of Coventry, exposed the family weakness for grammar and spelling, and made him the laughing stock of his intellectual acquaintances. 'I doubt I ever met with so obtuse a man before,' wrote Harriet Martineau, 'He goes about like a chuckling detective on the track of a swindler.'[21]

Charles Holte Bracebridge touched the lives of two of the greatest Englishwomen of all time. Sometimes they were irritated by him, and occasionally angered, but the ill feeling did not persist. George Eliot forgave Mr Brooke's shortcomings, and allowed him to live 'to a good old age', visited regularly by his family.

Florence Nightingale was also generous in her tribute. After Bracebridge's death in 1872, she wrote, 'I never enjoyed any time in my life so much as my time at Rome'. And of the Crimea, she added, that Bracebridge was, 'The only man in all England who would have lived with willingness such a "pigging" life.' Despite the problems he had caused her, Nightingale's affection for him remained undiminished. He was, she said, 'The kindest of friends and the best and noblest of men. All his life he was fighting battles against cruelty and oppression.'[22]

In his home town, too, Bracebridge was remembered with affection. The hatters whom he had helped made their own modest tribute. In 1905, Charles Vero, now an old man, wrote to the local newspaper to ask why there was, in Atherstone, no memorial to the Bracebridges. A plain obelisk now stands in the town cemetery, inscribed simply with the dates of birth and death of Charles Holte Bracebridge and his wife, Selina. It is an unpretentious monument with nothing of the flamboyance and ornament which characterises the memorials of most well-to-do Victorians. Nothing else remains of the Bracebridges in Atherstone, save their name. Their home is gone, replaced by an estate of indifferent houses, and nothing remains to connect them with the trade they brought to the small market town.

---

[21] Haight, p. 291.
[22] Woodham-Smith, p. 530.

Postscript

THE LAST HUNDRED YEARS have seen a gradual decline in Atherstone as a hatting centre, despite the fact that it remains today the only place in Great Britain where wool felt hoods are manufactured. From the 1890s when most of the town's population had some connection with the trade, until the 1990s, when fewer than 200 people were employed in hatting, the vagaries of fashion, politics and economics have taken their toll. Since the hatters began to flex their collective muscle in the first quarter of the nineteenth century there were signs that labour relations would become a major issue. The independent nature of the hatter was not cowed by the factory system. It was still possible, even in more recent years, to find hatters absent from their work bench after the weekend as they celebrated 'Hatters' Monday', a tradition which had its precedent in craft industries elsewhere. Wrangles over wage rates were approached with foreboding by the factory masters, and news that a garret [1] was in progress was often enough to strike fear into the hearts of all but the toughest of them.

The 1880s had been troubled years. A slump in the trade caused by the onset of political turbulence in the Balkans, which cut off a lucrative market, had tightened up employment and threatened the stability of the local industry. In response to the growing local strength of the unions, in 1891 the employers formed the Warwickshire Felt Hat Manufacturers Association. Within a year the industry was embroiled in the worst strike of its history, with rifts developing between the manufacturers as some took their own line in attempting to settle the dispute.

The legacy of this strike was a long and devastating depression which took the trade into the twentieth century considerably weakened. Furthermore, it was a fearfully competitive trade, in a world market, with exports always subject to the whims of the importing countries and their capricious governments. Later, more financial pressure came to bear upon

---

[1] Meeting of workers in which a ballot was held to decide who should take a contentious issue to the factory master.

the surviving factories, as they faced increasing government legislation. Modern health and safety standards, employment protection, pollution and building control, and fire regulations, all had to be paid for out of falling profits.

Profits were never healthy enough to finance the research and development needed to mechanise hatmaking so that it met modern expectations. However, the industry was never short of ideas. All over the world, ever since machinery was invented, hatters had been seeking the magic formula which would enable them to feed wool into a machine and mysteriously create a felt hood, without human intervention. Patent libraries are littered with their vain attempts. As early as 1859 Charles Vero and James Everitt patented a machine which transformed wool into hardened forms without handling, but like all subsequent attempts, it was without success. Even in today's technological world, the magic formula continues to elude the hatters. The wool still needs to pass through at least a dozen pairs of hands, resting between processes, before it becomes a hat. Hatting remains a craft industry.

Despite all these difficulties, Atherstone still retained its place as a major manufacturing centre for wool felt hats. As is evident from photographs of local gatherings, almost everyone wore a hat. Furthermore, no man, either employee or visitor, would be allowed over the threshold of a hat factory without a hat on his head. Besides being a form of protection, the hat was a mark of office, or an emblem of status. But as the years passed the hat began to lose its importance. Since feltmaking came into this country, in the time of Queen Elizabeth I, it has always been subject to the fluctuations of fashion and economics, and the boom after the Second World War was no exception. Every demobbed serviceman was issued with a hat. But men had been forced to wear uniform hats throughout the War, and given the freedom of peace, they no longer wished to wear them. To protect their heads from the weather they might still wear the occasional trilby, but not for long. Car ownership was growing and people spent less time exposed to the elements. The need to wear a hat had passed, and it returned to being a mark of status, or an item of leisure wear.

For women, hats became fashion accessories. Mini-booms came and went, usually led by royalty. Princess Elizabeth and Princess Diana had only to be photographed in a particular hat, for it to be reproduced by the thousand and sold in chain stores across the world. But these booms and troughs did little for the trade in general, and overall it declined steadily so that, by the 1970s, in Atherstone, only three factories remained – Denham & Hargrave (later Austin Aspden), Vero & Everitt, and Wilson & Stafford.

In 1986, under the leadership of a new managing director, Wilson & Stafford, bought Austin Aspden Limited. Then, in 1987, when it became obvious that only one company could survive and prosper, the owners of Vero & Everitt Limited agreed to sell the major part of their hatting business to Wilson & Stafford Limited, controlled by their cousins and former rivals. Today Wilson & Stafford, which occupies a canalside site in Atherstone, is the last remaining wool felt hat factory in Britain, and one of a very few left in the world.

Warwickshire Hatters

photographs by Ian Beesley;
introduction and commentary by Judy Vero

Warwickshire Hatters is a photographic record of the last days of feltmaking at Vero & Everitt, the oldest of Atherstone's hat factories to survive into the 1980s. The fifty-three black and white photograph are by Lancashire's Ian Beesley, whose images have been described by film producer Sir David Puttnam as 'very, very original'. Step by step, Beesley takes the reader through the many processes of a craft industry which has its roots in medieval times. The machinery, the materials and the hatters themselves are seen in a working environment which owes little to the accustomed standards of the late twentieth century.

'Beesley's photographs reveal remarkably antiquated work conditions housing happy faces and skilled hands'
Chris Dickie, *British Journal of Photography*

'His photographs are not morbid or funereal; they are a celebration of what was once great, providing a record of people, places and traditions for future generations to enjoy.'
Eamonn McCabe, The Guardian

Published by Ryburn.   ISBN 1-85331-088-5

copies obtainable from:
Vero & Everitt Ltd, Station Street, Atherstone, CV9 1BZ